A Companion to John Dewey's *Democracy and Education*

A Companion to John Dewey's *Democracy and Education*

D. C. PHILLIPS

The University of Chicago Press ❁ *Chicago and London*

The University of Chicago Press, Chicago 60637
The University of Chicago Press, Ltd., London

Printed in the United States of America

25 24 23 22 21 20 19 18 17 16   1 2 3 4 5

ISBN-13: 978-0-226-40823-1 (cloth)
ISBN-13: 978-0-226-40837-8 (paper)
ISBN-13: 978-0-226-40840-8 (e-book)
DOI: 10.7208/chicago/9780226408408.001.0001

Library of Congress Cataloging-in-Publication Data

Names: Phillips, D. C. (Denis Charles), 1938– author. | Guide to (work): Dewey, John, 1859–1952. Democracy and education.
Title: A companion to John Dewey's Democracy and education / D. C. Phillips.
Description: Chicago ; London : University of Chicago Press, 2016. | Includes bibliographical references.
Identifiers: LCCN 2016009663 | ISBN 9780226408231 (cloth : alkaline paper) | ISBN 9780226408378 (paperback : alkaline paper) | ISBN 9780226408408 (e-book)
Subjects: LCSH: Dewey, John, 1859–1952. Democracy and education. | Education—Philosophy. | Education—Social aspects.
Classification: LCC LB875.D5 P52 2016 | DDC 370.1—dc23 LC record available at http://lccn.loc.gov/2016009663

♾ This paper meets the requirements of ANSI/NISO Z39.48-1992 (Permanence of Paper).

"Companion": . . . someone or something that matches or goes with another; information booklet.

« WEBSTER »

Everyman, I will go with thee, and be thy guide,
In thy most need to go by thy side

« From the medieval morality play *Everyman* »

Contents

Introduction: John Dewey and Me

I first met John Dewey in 1958, some six years after his death. It was a brief encounter, and it was far from auspicious. I was a newly minted graduate in the sciences at the University of Melbourne, Australia, undertaking a yearlong program to become a qualified high school science teacher, and one of the required courses was a survey of great figures in the history of educational thought. And there he was—a far from imposing figure whose photograph reminded me of President Harry Truman, and his writings were quite incomprehensible. How, for example, could a (very) young biology-teacher-in-training glean much from the following passage from chapter 20 of *Democracy and Education* (1916): "The interest in experience as a means of basing truth upon objects, upon nature, led to looking at the mind as purely receptive. . . . For the mind to take a hand, so to speak, would be for it in the very process of knowing to vitiate true knowledge—to defeat its own purpose. The ideal was a maximum of receptivity." It was only much later that I came to comprehend this point. I also recall assiduously pouring over, all those years ago, the summaries that Dewey provided at the end of each chapter of this book—no doubt in an attempt to be helpful to his readers. Unfortunately, at the time they merely added to my bemusement. I felt the need for a guiding hand, for a companion—but alas, none was forthcoming.*

The situation was not quite so bleak as the reflections above might make it seem. I had taken a yearlong course in history and philosophy of science as part of my undergraduate studies, and the major focus of my degree had been in biology, with a strong emphasis on vertebrate anatomy, physiology, and evolution—and I was amazed to find that this background provided an entrée to Dewey. By a strange quirk of fate Dewey had been born in the very same year in which was published the book that was perhaps of greatest influence on him. For 1859 saw the arrival of both Dewey and Darwin's *Origin of Species*. This link between Dewey and me leapt out as I read the short preface to *Democracy and Education* (a matter that I will discuss in more detail after a few preliminary issues have been attended to).

After my year of teacher training, I was too busy learning how to survive in the classroom to pursue this nascent interest in Dewey, and to be frank, a great disincentive was the bad impression I had formed of him as an English-language stylist. After a few years, however, my view of him started to change when I came across a passage, in brilliant prose, that threw light on an experience I had undergone during my teacher training. The program at the University of Melbourne had an interesting structure: a month or so of lectures and seminars at the university, followed by a three-week "teaching round" during which us trainees

* When I was close to finishing the manuscript of the present book, I discovered that an earlier companion did, indeed, exist. Written by Herman Harrell Horne in the early 1930s, it had not found its way to Melbourne. Inevitably the passage of time has rendered some of it outdated; and obviously it could not take advantage of the major works Dewey produced in the last two decades of his life. I discuss Horne's companion in more detail in the bibliographical essay; and I have inserted references to the book at appropriate places in my text, for in some instances his views are diametrically opposed to my own—and thus he keeps me "honest."

went out to teach, under supervision, in a high school; this was followed by another period of work at the university, which in turn was followed by another teaching round. My memory is that there were three such cycles in total, and the three schools to which we were sent were deliberately varied; the range included academically oriented schools, private schools with both boarders and day students, Catholic schools, schools in tough urban settings, and so on. The experience that was so memorable for me occurred on the first day of my second teaching round.

I had been posted to a prestigious private school of venerable age (in England, by some perverse foible of the English language, this would have been called a greater public school), and on my first morning I followed my assigned "master teacher" to observe him at work with a class that I would be teaching for the next three weeks. The classroom was horrendous! It probably had been state of the art at the end of the nineteenth century, with its very small desks screwed firmly to the floor—and adding to the horror was the fact that I had to squeeze my almost six-foot frame into one of them at the back of the room. And there I sat for almost an hour, praying that fire did not break out, for I knew that I would never be able to escape in time. Here is the passage from Dewey that I found so enlightening; it had been written many decades earlier, for chapter 2 of *The School and Society* (1900/1915), about the time the classroom that so horrified me was built:

> Just as the biologist can take a bone or two and reconstruct the whole animal, so, if we put before the mind's eye the ordinary schoolroom, with its rows of ugly desks placed in geometrical order, crowded together so that there shall be as little moving room as possible, desks almost all of the same size, with just space enough to hold books, pencils, and paper, and add a table, some chairs, the bare walls, and possibly a few pictures, we can reconstruct the only educational activity that can possibly go on in such a place. It is all made "for listening"—because simply studying lessons out of a book is only another kind of listening; it marks the dependency of one mind upon another.

Made for listening! What an insight—not made for working in, or to facilitate active inquiry, or even to allow communication with fellow learners. Students were effectively forced into the role of *spectators*. I found that Dewey had further insights about this in *Democracy and Education*, as we will see later.

In the years that followed, I discovered more passages, also in impressive prose, that threw light on my classroom teaching experiences; and furthermore, some of the originally murky passages began to move into focus. I realized they were expressing important and extremely interesting, though often debatable, philosophical insights about matters such as how humans gain reliable knowledge, the mind in its relation to the body, the relation between the individual and his or her community, and how moral progress can occur. Throughout, however, I refrained from romanticizing Dewey—and to be frank, some passages in his writings remain murky after half a century of study, and sometimes his arguments seem weak or even malformed. But after all, Dewey was human.

I embarked on deeper study of philosophy and the history of educational thought at the University of Melbourne, and eventually wrote a master's thesis on the different ways in which Herbert Spencer (the influential nineteenth-century British essayist) and Dewey used the theory of evolution; and in 1968 I earned my doctorate for a dissertation on the ways in which holist or organicist ideas (originating in Hegel's philosophy) played out in Dewey's writings. The struggles to be clear and precise in this dissertation on a difficult topic made me sympathetic to the struggles Dewey must have had in attempting to be clear when formulating his philosophy, and I was prepared to live with some defective passages in his writings. In 1974 I left Australia to take up a position at Stanford, where for many years I taught a course (listed both in the Graduate School of Education and the Department of Philosophy) titled "The Philosophical and Educational Thought of John Dewey."

Over the passing years, I accumulated a number of different editions of *Democracy and Education* (hereafter usually referred to as D&E). This book was the centerpiece of my courses; it had been written in 1915 and first published in 1916, and was (and is still) regarded by many scholars as Dewey's major work in an impressive corpus of about forty books and eight hundred essays and papers. My copies of D&E gradually became filled with marginal notes written in pencil that accumulated as I worked with my Stanford students. At some point I realized that these notes constituted the skeleton for a companion to *Democracy and Education*—the work that I had so much desired all those decades ago.

Why a Companion?

Up to this point, I have suggested that it is the difficulty of much, but certainly not all, of Dewey's prose that makes it useful to have assistance in unraveling matters. In general, as many commentators have remarked, Dewey was not a good writer, but it must also be noted that he wrote D&E when he was in his midfifties, and his prose style had matured long before, in the closing decade or two of the nineteenth century. As a result, there are many passages that seem ponderous and pose difficulty for the reader in the twenty-first century—although it also has been noted that there are some scattered passages in his works that read like rousing "lay sermons." Herman Harrell Horne, in the companion to D&E that he wrote in 1932, pulls no punches when he elaborates on the stylistic difficulty of Dewey's prose:

> the use of familiar words with unfamiliar meanings; the use of words with pregnant meanings; the use of long, involved, and highly concentrated sentences . . . ; the development of different important ideas in the same paragraph; and not making it clear when he is stating the views of others and when his own. . . . In addition, Dr. Dewey, like Browning, knows and takes for granted in his references as known so much history which his readers do not know and which future followers of his pragmatic educational theories are likely to know less and less. (pp. xiii–xiv)

There is enough here to justify writing a companion!

However, there are three additional reasons why it is a good idea not to make the journey into *Democracy and Education* alone. First, the book is a century old; and while this is cause for celebration, it is also a source of difficulty—for some of the issues that Dewey discusses are ones that we are no longer familiar with. Some help may be required to fully comprehend the point of some of Dewey's discussions.

Second, at several places in the book Dewey puts forward a revolutionary way of thinking about the topic in hand—he turns the conventional approach on its head. And this can be quite puzzling for the reader who, quite naturally, is approaching the topic with the conventional conceptual equipment. For example, in several chapters toward the middle of the book Dewey rejects the traditional way of thinking about *thinking*. Without stealing the thunder from my (and Dewey's) later and more detailed discussions, it is safe to say that most of us approach the topic of "thinking" with the assumption (the self-evident assumption!) that it is a mental process that takes place inside one's head. Rodin's famous statue *The Thinker* is the classical epitome of this; he is sitting quietly in deep reflection, alone, without pen or paper or electronic tablet, even without clothes. It is clear that he is, indeed, *thinking*. But as we will see later in this companion, Dewey will have none of this!

Third, Dewey—although a scholar of great learning—only very rarely made use of the usual scholarly mechanisms of citations and direct quotations (in the entire—and lengthy—volume he only mentions seven sources); so again it is useful to have at hand a companion to provide some of the scholarly context of Dewey's discussions. An interesting example of this issue is his treatment of the philosophical tradition to which he clearly belonged when D&E was written—he was a pragmatist, yet this term is only referenced twice in the index to the book, and the two great founding figures of this philosophical movement, C. S. Peirce and William James, are not referenced at all (although James is named within the volume). The fact of the matter was that Dewey had taken a course in logic from Peirce, and in various other writings he acknowledged the great inspiration

James had been for him (and James in turn had been inspired by Peirce).

Finally, it is interesting to note in passing that another great twentieth-century philosopher, whose influence is often regarded as comparable to that of Dewey—namely, Ludwig Wittgenstein—also avoided notes and quotations; the philosopher Max Black did a great service by writing *A Companion to Wittgenstein's "Tractatus,"* which helped fill in the scholarly gaps.

The Structure of This Companion

There are at least two essential features that must be possessed by a genuine companion. First, he, she, or it should be with you at every stage of the journey. A companion who disappears at crucial points is a sham, a fair-weather friend. This will not be the case here; this particular companion will contain discussions of every chapter of D&E in the order in which they appear in the original. And just as D&E opens with a brief preface, so will this companion open with a discussion of this short two-paragraph item.

The second essential feature for a companion is that he, she, or it should be interesting. A boring companion will not be with you very long before a parting of the ways! Hence in this companion the style—to the degree possible—is straightforward and conversational in tone. Furthermore, perhaps nothing is more tedious for a reader entering new territory (especially territory as initially daunting as D&E might seem) than to be confronted many times in each paragraph by detailed scholarly notes and references that at their worst can be incredibly cumbersome—it is a strange intellect that is turned on by prose that is characterized by frequent use of "ibid," "op. cit.," "Dewey, *Middle Works*, vol. 14, p. 34," and the like. This is particularly a problem for a discussion of D&E; there now is a "standard" edition published by Southern Illinois University Press, a volume that is merely one among several dozen that constitute its Collected Works of John Dewey series. But there are many other editions of D&E available in circulation, in libraries, and on the web. Unfortunately, because of differences in type size and layout, and the length of an editor's introduction, the pagination of these editions is surprisingly different. And, as I discovered in my Stanford classes, nothing is more aggravating than having one person referring to a passage on page 20 when this passage does not appear on page 20 of the edition used by others, or on page 19 or page 21. (A concrete example is the quotation from chapter 20 given at the outset. I possess three different editions of D&E, and this passage appears on page 276, page 312, and pages 267–68!) Having no control over which edition of D&E each reader of this companion uses, I wish to avoid this type of annoyance, and therefore in draconian fashion I do not cite the page numbers at all, but simply refer to the chapter, and occasionally to the approximate location within the chapter, of the passage being discussed. This should not be the source of serious problems for, after all, the reader should be reading a copy of D&E (*any* copy of it) alongside this companion—this is the whole point. To aid interested readers in pursuing topics in more depth, however, I do include at the very end of the volume a brief bibliographical essay.

Cautionary Note

There is a final, very important message to the reader before the journey into D&E commences: This volume is a *companion*, and not a *summary* or *replacement*. Its purpose is to provide pointers, background, help, and commentary pointing out issues that interested readers need to pursue further for themselves. This book is not intended to offer, and does not provide, a précis of *Democracy and Education* that one can read in place of the original. Rather, it is meant to make the journey of discovery into this remarkable book even more fruitful than it would be if undertaken alone. Furthermore, like many journeys into foreign territory, progress will be a tad easier if the reader has a sense of the terrain in advance—it is a good idea to read or at least scan each chapter of D&E before using the guidebook.

Acknowledgements

Over the decades, my exploration of Dewey's work has been enriched by comments from colleagues and students on several continents. Barbara Falk and Elizabeth Gasking, of the University of Melbourne, guided my early efforts at scholarly writing on Dewey; my colleague at Monash University in Melbourne, the historian John Cleverley, with whom I taught for several years, provided insight into the background of nineteenth-century ideas; at Stanford on a number of occasions I led a seminar on Dewey with my colleague Nel Noddings; and a number of doctoral students—now colleagues—wrote dissertations on Dewey from which I have profited. International visitors to Stanford also contributed to my education, especially James Marshall from New Zealand and Johannes Bellman from Germany. Eric Bredo, most lately at Toronto, enriched my understanding of James, Mead, and Peirce; and Deborah Kerdeman at the University of Washington, Seattle, has increased my tolerance of Continental philosophy. My colleagues at Stanford, Ray McDermott and Eamonn Callan, provided provocative insights on a variety of matters pertaining to Dewey. And of course there have been several generations of students who have taken my courses and who have raised challenging issues. Finally, my greatest debt is to my wife, Valerie, who read every word in this book (several times) and who increased its clarity and also reduced the number of commas, parentheses, and exclamation marks!

The Companion to *Democracy and Education: An Introduction to the Philosophy of Education*

Preface, 1915

There are many readers, no doubt of reckless or impatient disposition, who make a habit of skipping past anything in a book that bears the title "Preface" or even "Introduction." They are overly keen to get embroiled in the "main work" as soon as possible. In the case of the preface to D&E this constitutes a major blunder. (And, it should be pointed out, it is an even greater mistake in the case of this companion!) For the first part of this two-paragraph piece that Dewey wrote in 1915 is only three sentences—albeit, in typical Dewey style, three long sentences—yet it contains the key not only to D&E but to much of Dewey's corpus. What a bargain: having the key to unlock dozens if not scores of books and essays, all in three sentences! It is worth savoring each of these in turn. (The following discussion bypasses the second and shorter paragraph containing Dewey's personal acknowledgements.)

The first, and shortest, sentence proclaims that the aim of D&E is to "detect and state" the "ideas implied in a democratic society" and to apply these ideas to educational problems. In using the terms "democratic" and "democracy" in referring to a society, Dewey is not pointing to the presence of a particular electoral mechanism (free elections) or to an electoral principle (one person, one vote). He has in mind something deeper, for to him the term implies a mode of living, a mode of interaction between the individuals who constitute a community. Dewey had memories, perhaps somewhat romanticized, of the New England state of Vermont in which he spent his childhood—of such things as decisions about matters of local import being made by citizens who were equals and who negotiated their differences at town meetings, and neighbors helping each other gather firewood or make candles in preparation for the coming harsh winter. Sometimes he used the term "conjoint living" to refer to all of this, for in this view there were many crisscrossing lines of connection or association between individuals. What are the educational implications of this conception of democracy? D&E is an attempt to provide an answer.

It probably is wise, even at this early stage, to alert the reader to the fact that although the account of democracy that Dewey gives is beguiling, it has been too "Pollyanna-like" for some. Does Dewey deal satisfactorily with the fact that sometimes in communities there are unnegotiable differences between individuals and that sometimes people act in self-serving ways rather than with the welfare of the community in mind? Does he deal satisfactorily with the fact that there are minority groups with discordant priorities? Does he sufficiently recognize that institutions exist that to a considerable extent shape or even determine what courses of action are possible? Or, perhaps, is Dewey putting such matters aside and offering a picture—an ideal—of what a democratic community should endeavor to become? Readers will have to decide such issues for themselves as progress is made through the chapters.

The second sentence, more complex in structure, is best quoted in full:

> The discussion includes an indication of the constructive aims and methods of public education as seen from this point of view, and a critical estimate of the theories of knowing and moral development which were formulated in earlier social conditions, but which still operate, in societies nominally democratic, to hamper the adequate realization of the democratic ideal.

The last two-thirds of this sentence summarizes a thesis Dewey only argues and defends cursorily in D&E, although he certainly makes use of it quite frequently, as we will note as our reading progresses; he also referred to it in other works but argued it most extensively in his readable volume *Reconstruction in Philosophy* (1920/1948). Stated in its most general and probably its most defensible form, this thesis holds that the ideas that are circulating within a society, even outmoded ones that still survive, can influence the practices and policies that are current in this society. In a more controversial form, his position was that the philosophical theories held at any historical stage of a society's development (and these of course included "theories of knowing and moral development") were a reflection of the pressures and problems and conditions that the society faced at that particular time—in a sense, Dewey can be interpreted as arguing that they were part of the society's adaptive response to its environment. While this is well and good, Dewey held it becomes a problem if the philosophies of a period, and the institutions and modes of social interaction, and so on, that were developed under their influence, persisted after the environment had undergone major change. For the persistence of the older ways and assumptions could prevent the development of new and more adaptive ideas, ideals, and practices. In short, the inheritance coming from earlier times will now "hamper the realization of the democratic ideal." For example, later in D&E we will find that Dewey identified the existence of the kind of antiquated educational arrangement displayed in the classroom I mentioned in the introduction (the one that had so horrified me) as a consequence of an old philosophical theory persisting when the social conditions that once had made it relevant no longer existed.

To dispel any suspicion that I am reading too much into a few lines of prose, and to substantiate that Dewey did, indeed, hold the thesis I have been discussing, here is a statement from Dewey's introduction to the 1948 edition of *Reconstruction in Philosophy*:

> The adverse criticisms of philosophies of the past are not directed at these systems with respect to their connection with intellectual and moral issues of their own time and place, but with respect to their relevancy in a much changed human situation. The very things that make the great systems objects of esteem and admiration in their own socio-cultural contexts are in large measure the very grounds that deprive them of "actuality" in a world whose main features are different.

It is fair to say that this view of the nature (and social origins and purpose) of philosophy is both very interesting and very controversial. While it is a truism that any philosophical position must have arisen in a social context, it is arguable that the form and content of this position is more a reflection of the state of debate and controversy within the philosophical tradition at the time than it is a reflection of the social issues that are prevalent. Furthermore, how on earth could it be established that a philosophical thesis was, indeed, a "reflection" of some aspect of the sociocultural environment? Again these are issues the reader should ponder. The discussion must now move on, but the issues raised here will resurface in the discussions of later chapters of D&E.

The third and final sentence of the paragraph under scrutiny reads as follows:

> As will appear from the book itself, the philosophy stated in this book connects the growth of democracy with the development of the experimental method in the sciences, evolutionary ideas in the biological sciences, and the industrial reorganization, and is concerned to point out the changes in subject matter and method of education indicated by these developments.

Dewey is simply whetting the reader's appetite here. The ideas he signals are complex and to some degree controversial, and they require much more exposition and argument to make them fully graspable—and obviously he could not do all of this work in the preface, which would then run amok and become the whole of the book! But certainly these snippets of an agenda are intriguing if not mind-boggling. For example, the experimental method of the sciences is a method for gathering evidence for or against the truth of a hypothesis, so what is the link here with democracy? And what has the evolutionary struggle for existence, and the survival of individuals with the fittest adaptations, to do with education? And to make these questions more intractable, what is to be made of Dewey's remark that the "industrial reorganization" needs to be included in the picture?

While all these matters are discussed (and perhaps resolved) in D&E, it probably is useful at the outset to give the reader at least a hint—an "advance organizer"—about the direction in which Dewey's book will take us. The key is an idea Dewey took from the great psychologist and cofounder of the philosophy of pragmatism William James, and possibly from others—namely, that the human ability to think (or, our possession of "mind") is an adaptive feature that evolved, and which had great survival value in the struggle for existence in the hostile environments in which our ancestors eked out their existence. The biological function of the ability to think, in other words, is that it is to be used to intelligently direct our behavior. Furthermore, this ability was acquired by our ancestors living in a social environment, not by solitary individuals living in caves (like primitive, solitary versions of Rodin's *Thinker*). The capacity to think was dependent on the existence of bodies of accumulated knowledge and experience and social tools such as language. All of this was captured in fine style in a passage in chapter 4 of Dewey's *The School and Society* (1900/1915); in contrast to earlier times,

> at present the tendency is to conceive individual mind as a function of social life—as not capable of operating or developing by itself, but as requiring continual stimulus from social agencies, and finding its nutrition in social supplies. The idea of heredity has made familiar the notion that the equipment of the individual, mental as well as physical, is an inheritance from the race: a capital inherited by the individual from the past and held in trust by him for the future. The idea of evolution has made familiar the notion that mind . . . developed in an environment which is social as well as physical.

When humans evolved the capacity to think, we also slowly developed intellectual tools or strategies—for example, about ways to test plans of action, and beliefs or hypotheses, to see whether they were likely to work if put into practice. The philosopher Karl Popper put this nicely when he noted that a great advance in human evolution occurred when we evolved the capacity to let our defective plans die in our place—a thing that the experimental method of testing makes possible, for it allows us to detect faulty plans and hypotheses in controlled or laboratory settings, and reject them without the catastrophe of having them fail when we are using them in some real-life setting. For this reason the experimental method is among the greatest of the tools that humans have devised—and it not only has made possible the great advances in our physical standard of living, but it also has the potential to strengthen the processes of decision and policy making that are essential in a modern democratic society.

It was the implications of this biological or evolutionary theory of mind lying at the core of Dewey's philosophy that made it so unpalatable to critics, and there seem to have been many of them in the years following the publication of D&E. Surely Horne was speaking for many when he penned the following assessment, which appears in his comments on Dewey's preface:

> Such a conception of philosophy is in line with the "Positivism" of August Comte and the "Agnosticism" . . . of Herbert Spencer. . . . This philosophy is also known as "Instrumentalism" because it uses thought not to go beyond experience but as an instrument or tool to find suitable means for ends with[in] experience. Since it subordinates thought to action, it is also called "Pragmatism." Since it locates values within the stream of human experience, it is also called "Humanism." And since it advocates the supremacy of the scientific method, it is also known as "Experimentalism." . . . Here we are to see a philosophy of education that raises no questions concerning the transcendent; that is, concerning the general meaning and issues of existence, the nature of reality, the explanation of the cosmos, or the place of man in the universe, and makes no suggestion whatever that education may in any way be concerned with any of these things. (pp. 2–3)

Of course, what Horne puts forward here as a criticism, others will consider a virtue. I leave it to the reader to determine, as we progress, to what degree (if any) the author of this companion shares Horne's sentiments in this feisty passage.

To return to Dewey: Where does "the industrial reorganization" come into the picture? Let it suffice, for now, to point out that the technological developments in modern societies resulted in the restructuring of industry in the Industrial Revolution, and the concomitant restructuring of society and of the social and occupational roles within it; and this meant that parallel changes needed to be made in education to keep it relevant to these new stresses and strains. If the human race was to survive, all of this needed to be handled with intelligence—and the need is still present, because the challenges are still with us. It remains to be seen whether Dewey's discussion in D&E points the way to survival.

Finally, a comment needs to be made about the date when this preface was written: August 1915. This was exactly one year after the outbreak of the Great War (WWI), and although the USA did not enter the fray until 1917, the bloodbath had begun and entry seemed inevitable. The *Lusitania* had been sunk, London had been bombed by Zepplins, Canadians had been gassed at Ypres, a submarine blockade of the British Isles had started, and the carnage in Flanders was underway. Yet there is no indication of any of this in the preface or in the book itself, which, given this horrendous context, has a certain ethereal quality to it. (To illustrate his theory of decision making in chapter 11, Dewey uses the example of a general in the "current war," but it is a thoroughly decontextualized discussion that, considering the situation in 1915, seems exceedingly pallid.) But Dewey was not the kind of man who was unaware of contemporary events; and he almost certainly judged them to constitute a major crisis—after all, a centerpiece of his position in philosophy was his view that the philosophy of a period must be relevant to the social issues of that time. And looking back at WWI later, he certainly saw that it ushered in an age of severe pessimism: "The First World War was a decided shock to the earlier period of optimism, in which there prevailed widespread belief in continued progress among peoples and classes, and hence a sure movement to harmony and peace. Today . . . (i)nsecurity and strife are so general that the prevailing attitude is one of anxious and pessimistic uncertainty" (introduction to *Reconstruction in Philosophy* [1948]).

So there is something of a mystery about the calm tone of D&E, although the book clearly enough makes the case that the aims, methods, and philosophical underpinnings of education are seriously outmoded and in urgent need of reformulation. As a corrective to what I see as this strange lacuna in D&E, I cannot resist quoting Woody Allen, whose memorable prose in "My Speech to the Graduates" pithily captures the challenge that faced educationists in 1916 and that still faces us today: "More than any other time in history, mankind faces a crossroads. One path leads to despair and utter hopelessness. The other to total extinction. Let us pray we have the wisdom to choose correctly."

1

Education as a Necessity of Life

From the dawn of recorded history down to the present age, human communities have been educating their youngsters, and gradually social roles and institutions and structures evolved to carry out this function. Indeed, for about the last 150 years the resources allocated to the task of education have been massive—think of the investments that have been made in establishing school and preschool systems, colleges and universities, libraries, teacher-training institutions, research units, policy development units, and even programs in philosophy of education. All of this is pretty much taken for granted, and many of us do not problematize the general phenomenon and ask why this is so. But if pressed for an answer, we give replies that usually reflect our social positions: if we are successful capitalists, we may be prone to see educational processes and institutions as providing a skilled workforce; if we are government bureaucrats, we see them as contributing to economic growth or international competitiveness; if we are elderly or infirm, we may regard education as a weapon against violence and lawlessness in society; if we are philosophers, we are as likely as not to see education as contributing to the development of the personal autonomy of students; and if we are political theorists, we might focus on educating students to undertake the responsibilities of citizenship.

In these opening pages of D&E, Dewey does not adopt any of these familiar perspectives. It has seemed to me, from my early days as a high school teacher of biology and then as a philosopher of social science, always with an interest in the theory of evolution, that Dewey is adopting in these pages the stance of an evolutionary biologist (a perspective he alerted us to in that fecund third sentence of the preface). For if in the course of doing fieldwork, the biologist comes across a specimen of interest, a specimen with several distinctive characteristics, he or she will seek to discover the *function* of these features—the contribution they make to increasing the probability of survival in the struggle for existence of that specimen's species. Without survival value, those features would have been highly unlikely to have evolved and certainly would not have persisted in the species for very long. Thus Dewey, in adopting this approach, regards communities, or social groups, as being in some sense units of evolution, and institutions and social practices as being the equivalent—in these social units—of the adaptive features that biological organisms acquire in the course of their evolution. Thus, to put it in a nutshell, when he looked at societies from a "biological perspective," he noticed that—among other things—they all had systems or schemes for educating their young, and he asked the question, What is the function, that has survival value, of educational institutions and practices? (In the interest of full disclosure, I should note here that this is a perspective that might, in some quarters, be received with skepticism, although personally I think it is not unreasonable and certainly can be very fruitful.)

Dewey's answer to this question is simple, and strangely moving, and it serves as a starting point for his discussions in D&E: there is a constant flow of individuals through a society, as members are born into it and others die out of it, yet the society survives and maintains its identity—and it is education that is responsible for this. In almost poetic prose, he puts the point this way near the end of the first section:

> The death of each of its constituent members is as certain as if an epidemic took them all at once. But the graded difference in age, the fact that some are born as some die, makes possible through transmission of ideas and practices the constant reweaving of the social fabric.

Isn't this an obvious point? Yes, he admits a few lines further on,

> so obvious, indeed, is the necessity of teaching and learning for the continued existence of a society that we may seem to be dwelling unduly on a truism. But justification is found in the fact that such emphasis is a means of getting us away from an unduly scholastic and formal notion of education.

Here Dewey also is making a point that has been followed up by many philosophers of education—namely, that "education" and "schooling" are not synonymous. Not everything that takes place in the formal institutions such as schools is educational, and everything educational does not take place in schools. And before societies became complex and developed formal educational roles and institutions, of course, informal education was the "only act in town."

In essence, then, armed with his evolutionary theoretical lens, Dewey offers us in chapter 1 a type of "foundation or creation myth." (He offers another one of these accounts, about the rise of the discipline of philosophy, in the early portions of *Reconstruction in Philosophy*, published a few years after D&E). In broad terms it goes as follows: Early human groups passed on such things as skills and local knowledge to their young members; this was done informally—primarily by the youngsters engaging in activities such as hunting or food gathering alongside the senior members of the group. The more of these kinds of things that were shared between the members of the group (skills, knowledge, group traditions, and so on), the more it became a community rather than just a group or collection of individuals. Processes of communication therefore were central in the formation of communities. As Dewey puts it, communities did not exist *by* communication; they existed *in* communication. "There is more than a verbal tie between the words common, community, and communication," Dewey wrote early in section 2. "Men live in a community in virtue of the things which they have in common; and communication is the way in which they come to possess things in common." (It may be giving too much of the future story away, but I cannot suppress the impulse to point out that later Dewey objects to teaching youngsters communication skills in settings that do not allow them to communicate! The now infamous classroom to which I keep referring is a case in point, for as Dewey put it, it was "made 'for listening.' ")

Dewey continues his account by arguing that eventually the material that needs to be transmitted becomes so complex that it is not viable to rely on informal means to impart it. Thus formal institutions and social roles "of direct tuition or schooling" evolve to serve this end, this function. As he puts it in section 3, "as civilization advances, the gap between the capacities of the young and the concerns of adults widens," and as a result, "ability to share effectively in adult activities thus depends upon a prior training given with this end in view." However, there is a danger here; a few paragraphs before the end of the chapter, Dewey issues a warning:

> But there are conspicuous dangers attendant upon the transition from indirect to formal education. Sharing in actual pursuit(s), whether directly or vicariously in play, is at least personal and vital. . . . Formal instruction, on the contrary, easily becomes remote and dead—abstract and bookish, to use the ordinary words of depreciation.

Once again the educational program suited for the horrendous classroom in which I did my practice teaching, all those years ago, comes to mind.

A final point needs to be made: Dewey nowhere denies that institutions or structures, ones that developed in order to fulfill a specific function that has survival value, can later acquire or can be given additional functions as well. Indeed he acknowledges this at the start of section 3, where he makes the point that social institutions first arise to serve some practical purpose but then can gradually acquire other functions—such as educational ones. And of course, educational institutions can acquire noneducational functions (such as becoming sites for delivery of free-meals programs, or places where students are "sorted" into different social classes). This phenomenon—a characteristic or structure that has one function coming to acquire additional functions or uses—is fairly common in biological evolution, so it was to be expected that something similar would be found to occur in social evolution. It is relevant to note that one of the important offshoots of the theory of evolution in the early decades of the twentieth century was the development of functionalism in psychology, sociology, and especially anthropology—an intellectual movement in which Dewey played an important role.

2

Education as a Social Function

The overall structure of this chapter is captured well enough in Dewey's summary at the end, where all seems straightforward—the theme, which leads on nicely from that of the first chapter, is the importance of the environment in developing within the young the "attitudes and dispositions necessary to the continuous and progressive life of a society." However, a journey can often be described as having been nonproblematic when it is over, when the difficulties and travails have faded from view (or have been suppressed deliberately); nevertheless the plain fact of life is that voyages are only rarely "plain sailing." And this, alas, is true of the journey Dewey takes us on in this early chapter.

The problems do not arise from the main theme, although why Dewey goes to such pains to stress the importance of the environment may not be clear to the reader and is a matter that needs to be addressed in due course. Rather, the problems come from the form of Dewey's arguments, which too often have a bewildering quality. For example, at several places he makes the point that knowledge cannot be imparted directly to students, but he does not define or illustrate with examples precisely what he means by this; perhaps he means "direct instruction" is not possible? But late in the chapter, he acknowledges that as societies develop complexity, the special environment of formal schooling evolves to serve a vital set of functions—and it seems clear that in courses in chemistry, physics, calculus, and so forth, direct instruction does occur and seems at least to be moderately efficacious. Furthermore, in chapter 12 Dewey acknowledges that ideas can be transferred from one person to another, but if not done properly (I discuss this later), they become—as he put it brilliantly—a "static, cold-storage ideal of knowledge." So it is not clear to the reader what Dewey is arguing in chapter 2, and one wishes that he could have been a tad more "user friendly" here! But perhaps I am introducing a difficulty into Dewey's work that does not really exist—perhaps, for some unknown reason, he is making the rather trivial point that we cannot (for example) extract a serum from Einstein's brain and inject it into students who thereby will suddenly (and "directly") know that $E = MC^2$. Once again, however, Dewey could have given us some help!

Another example, illustrative of a common foible in Dewey's style of argumentation, is to be found early in the chapter, in the middle of the very first paragraph. His argument opens with a sentence of some charm: "By various agencies, unintentional and designed, a society transforms uninitiated and seemingly alien beings into robust trustees of its own resources and ideals." So far, so good. But the following sentence introduces the mystery: "Education is thus a fostering, a nurturing, a cultivating process." It is the word "thus" that is highly problematic here; it indicates that the claim that follows this word is a consequence—a logical consequence—of the facts alluded to in the previous sentence. In other words, Dewey is claiming that it logically follows that education *must* be a fostering, nurturing, and cultivating process. But this simply is wrong; it does not follow at all. Indeed, the premise (that a society uses various agencies to transform the young into robust trustees of its resources and ideals) is quite compatible with the radically different conclusion that "therefore" education is a molding, shaping, and inculcating process. One cannot help entertaining the thought that it would have been more straightforward for Dewey to replace "thus" with a term that really captures the hidden structure of his argument—"abracadabra!"

The point is a logical one, and it is not being argued that Dewey is wrong in claiming that education should be considered a fostering, nurturing, cultivating process. This claim of Dewey's is a normative one—education *should* be thought of this way; and as such it is a claim that requires a substantial warranting case to be presented in its support. And this is precisely what Dewey offers in many of the later chapters of D&E, and in many of his other educational writings. So, at the *end* of D&E, but not at the outset, Dewey would (perhaps) have been justified in writing, "*Thus* it follows, from the case presented in this book, that education is a . . ." And so we must venture onward to determine whether Dewey indeed was justified!

Venturing onward brings us face-to-face with the importance Dewey assigns to the roles the environment plays in education (the environment being whatever enters into an organism's activity as a "sustaining or frustrating condition"). In this chapter of D&E, Dewey gives the reader little or no inkling of the evolutionary thought or the developments in psychology that helped frame his thinking on this matter. (It is worth mentioning, as an aside, that Dewey was not only a philosopher but also a psychologist—and enough of one to be elected president of the young American Psychological Association in 1899.)

The theory of evolution holds that all living organisms inhabit an environment and survive by making use of some of the resources it provides. But, of course, the environment sometimes (or always) has hostile elements, thus producing a struggle for existence. Organisms within a species have natural variation, and individuals with variations that are advantageous in this struggle have a greater chance of surviving and passing on their favorable variations to their offspring. It is this process of struggle, variation, selection, and differential survival that drives evolution. All of this occurs at the biological level, but the environment also plays an important role in shaping the behavioral repertoire of organisms—a matter addressed by several schools of psychology that emerged post–*Origin of Species*. For example, the behavior-ism of E. L. Thorndike, Dewey's colleague at Teachers College, held that if the environment in which an animal performed an action yielded a rewarding consequence (such as the obtaining of food), then that action would more likely be repeated when the stimulating circumstances were similar. (Later this was called "operant conditioning" by B. F. Skinner, who held that the process was responsible for shaping much of animal—including human—behavior.)

When it is the behavior of the human organism that is the focus, particularly the behavior of the youngsters of our species, the *social* environment becomes especially important. "The particular medium in which an individual exists," Dewey writes in the third paragraph of chapter 2, "leads him to see and feel one thing rather than another; it leads him to have certain plans in order that he may act successfully with others." In a social environment, an individual cannot "perform his own activities without taking the activities of others into account." But more than this—the developing individual must become a *partner*, and the activity must be what Dewey calls a *conjoint* or genuinely shared one. In short, the individual must come to care about the activity and its outcome the way others care about it, and then indeed it is *social*. Language is a vital tool here, but more than this—learning a language and using it are *themselves* conjoint social activities. (And, importantly, learning and using signs—the precursors of language—were related to the very acquisition of the human mind, as argued by Dewey's close friend and one-time colleague George Herbert Mead.)

To put it pithily, in a way which Dewey would likely endorse: our human forebears did not first acquire the ability to communicate, which then enabled them to become social animals; our ancestors were social animals and thus, simultaneously, were able to develop and refine the ability to communicate. For Dewey, whose thinking here was influenced by the German philosopher Hegel, the relation between an organism (including a human in-dividual) and the environment was not a linear one, not—as he called it later—an interaction; rather it was a transactional relation in which the environment influenced the individual organism and at the same time this individual influenced the environment. Or, put another way, the organism and its environment form a system, the parts of which are related holistically, organically, or dynamically. This is as true of the transactional relationship between humans and their social environments as it is of the relation between all animals and their respective environments. Pithier by far than Dewey's formulation of the point in this chapter, published in 1916, was the way he put it almost twenty years earlier when he wrote, in his famous short statement "My Pedagogic Creed,"

> I believe that the individual who is to be educated is a social individual and that society is an organic union of individuals. If we eliminate the social factor from the child we are left only with an abstraction; if we eliminate the individual factor from society, we are left only with an inert and lifeless mass.

So how does Dewey wind all of this up in the final half of the chapter? There is no great mystery here, for his exposition is relatively straightforward. He discusses the way in which the social medium acts to affect "every fiber of character and mind" of developing youngsters; he makes the point that unless developing individuals come to share the social attitudes toward the activities they are learning to participate in, then they are being trained like animals but not being educated; he points out that schools as institutions come into being when "social traditions are so complex that a considerable part of the social store is committed to writing and transmitted through written symbols . . . which cannot be picked up in accidental intercourse with others"; and schools acquire several functions—they simplify, out of all the complex material available, what is to be transmitted to the next generation; they pass on only those things that are deemed to be worthy; and finally, they act as a medium through which individuals, in effect, can widen their horizons and escape from the limitations of the social (sub)group into which they were born.

It is difficult to avoid concluding that in this chapter Dewey was engaged in an early (and perhaps pioneering) discussion of the process of *socialization* of new members of society, a discussion taken up by modern sociologists who have built on this promising start and have elucidated further, largely through empirical study, the effects (both intended and unintended), that schools have on those who attend them and those who work in them.

3

Education as Direction

For many years I did much of my scholarly writing (and reading of John Dewey) at my family's lakeside retreat somewhat north of the famed California wine-growing region of Napa Valley. We usually drove there by way of backroads that wound through the vineyards, and we marveled at the seasonal changes, especially those that took place over the course of a couple of years at places where new vines had been planted. (The spread of phylloxera necessitated that some growers remove all their mature vines, and after waiting for a few years replant their fields.) The young vines, although small, were not of exactly the same size, and for many months the rows in which they had been planted had a straggly appearance with little branches going hither and yon. But then the guiding hands of the field-workers took effect, order or rather direction was imposed on growth, and lo the vines all became alike, with the same height and shape. Tending to the growth of commercial plant crops is, indeed, a matter of imposing firm, external direction on the natural process of development. This lesson became clear to us on those occasions when, on our drive, we happened to pass a field of mature vines that had been abandoned; for when the firm guiding hands of the grower and field-workers were absent, the rows of plants again became disorderly—each vine seemingly following its own whim as to how to develop.

In chapter 3 Dewey argues that the early education of the developing child is also a matter of directing or guiding the natural process of development. As he puts it in the summary, "The natural or native impulses of the young do not agree with the life-customs of the group into which they were born. Consequently they have to be directed or guided." Some of this guidance is provided by physical and biological stimuli in the environment; and some comes from the authoritarian imposition of direction by parents and others. Like the plants in a vineyard, individuals can be guided or directed so that they act in orderly ways, but these ways mostly are not sustainable when the external forces are removed. Another way in which direction of development occurs in human groups is by the process of imitation, although Dewey argues it is of much more limited applicability than its proponents believe (of which, more a little later). But while all these factors can be effective in imposing some direction onto development (and in inhibiting growth and behavior that lead in other directions), these forms of guidance or direction are by no means sufficient to form and sustain a group that is in any sense a social community. (The neat and orderly vines are only a group or collection and are not such a community.)

In several places throughout the chapter, Dewey reveals the most effective, genuinely social means of direction or shaping of the child. Perhaps his simplest account is the one, located in the middle of the long section 2, in which he uses the example of teaching a child to bow as a means of showing respect:

> A child might be made to bow every time he met a certain person by pressure on his neck muscles, and bowing would finally become automatic. It would not, however, be an act of recognition or deference on his part, till he did it with a certain end in view—as having a certain meaning. And not till he knew what he was about and performed the act for the sake of its meaning could he be said to be "brought up" or educated to act in a certain way.

In later years many philosophers (building on Dewey) have made the point more strongly: unless what the child was doing was being done *because* of its meaning, it was not an *act* or *action* at all, but rather a *behavior* on a par with the behavior of a trained or conditioned animal. And it is worth noting that a similar point can be made about learning subject-matter content in school subjects. For example, a student can learn to recite Newton's first law of motion when asked to do so, but this is merely a mechanical response, a behavior, unless the student understands the meaning of this law and knows how—and why—to use it. The former case is one in which training has occurred, but the second—involving understanding of meaning—is a case of genuine education. In addition, it is also widely agreed nowadays that what precisely an action *is* can only be determined via its meaning. Thus, a child in class raises his or her arm—is this a greeting to a friend, a stretching of muscles, or an indication of the desire to ask a question? Only ascertaining the meaning can identify which of these characterizes the action. (This is one of the background beliefs of the field of ethnography—the pursuit of which, alas, would take us too far afield.)

But there is more that Dewey wants to tell us in chapter 3; he continues, at the end of the bowing example:

> To have the same ideas about things which others have, to be like-minded with them, and thus to be really members of a social group, is therefore to attach the same meanings to things and to acts which others attach. Otherwise, there is no common understanding, and no community life. But in a shared activity, each person refers what he is doing to what the other is doing, and *vice-versa*.

The explication of the nature of a community that Dewey is presenting here is important; clearly he was onto something—and furthermore, this conception keeps resurfacing in his writings (including many places in D&E). And so it is worth lingering over an illustrative example—but first, several clarificatory points need to be made about Dewey's usage of terms. He uses "community" and "social groups" in a very broad way, not only to refer to large entities like the "American community" and the "Stanford community," but also to refer to smaller groups that are found within these—such as a Stanford a cappella singing group or a New England township historical society. And when he refers to "ideas" or "meanings," his usage is similarly broad, encompassing purposes, intentions, aims or goals, beliefs, taken-for-granted assumptions, social rules and norms, ideals, plans for future action, and much more besides. And now we can turn to the example.

Consider a group of people playing or about to play a game—cricket, for example, or perhaps its inferior American cousin, baseball. If some members of this group are foreigners with no prior knowledge of the game, they might quickly be able to mimic the actions of the other players after watching a few demonstration games, or by following simple orders given to them by a coach ("try to catch the ball," "try to hit the ball if it seems to be in reach"). But if they lack understanding of the game (its aims or purposes, the roles of the various participants, the significance—the *meaning*—of the movements of the players on the field, the main strategies used by the offense and the defense), they cannot coordinate their actions with those of the other players—and so they cannot really be said to be playing the game, which is, in effect, to participate in a "conjoint activity." They certainly do not constitute a *team*, which is a small social community. In Dewey's words near the end of the chapter, they are not "engaging in a joint activity, where one person's use of material and tools is consciously referred to the use other persons are making of their capacities and appliances." There is "no common understanding, and [thus] no community life," as he put it earlier in the chapter.

There are other points made in the chapter, of course; prominent among these is the now familiar issue of the importance of language use in contexts where communication about shared activity is essential to success. And there is the issue of the shaping of development using the mechanism of imitation. Given the discussion above, on the importance in social interactions of understanding meanings, Dewey's position is not hard to comprehend. When one is learning by imitating, one is learning by focusing on external or observable features of the object, but one is not thereby learning to comprehend its *meaning* (in the broad sense of this term discussed earlier). Thus, no doubt you can learn to imitate what it is like to be undergoing existential doubt by posing in the manner of Rodin's *Thinker*; but no matter how well you perform the mimicry, you will not thereby learn what it is to suffer from existential doubt. The learner, as Dewey put it near the end of section 3, "imitates the means of doing, not the end [or purpose or meaning] or thing to be done." And he suggests a little later that in using mimicry, we are more than likely treating the learners like "apes, monkeys, parrots, or copy cats."

4

Education as Growth

This important chapter introduces a central concept in Dewey's educational pantheon, namely, the concept of growth, which he proceeds to use in giving an account of the nature (and especially the goals) of education. There is a link here, of course, with the topic of direction or guidance of development covered in the previous chapter, but Dewey does not do much by way of preparing the reader for the appearance of "education as growth," nor does he alert us to the considerable historical background. The present chapter also is noteworthy for another reason—it contains the first notes to appear in D&E, but neither of them is particularly informative.

The chapter opens with a five-paragraph discussion of the fact that a condition for growth is immaturity. As chance would have it, a few days before writing this commentary I happened to view a television documentary about the lives of pelicans, reference to which can illustrate the points Dewey is making. When the young pelicans hatch, they are featherless, they cannot fly, they cannot swim, they cannot gather food for themselves, and they depend on regurgitated mush from their parents. In short, the chicks are immature. Judged from the standpoint of the adult pelicans, they are lacking—they are without a variety of powers, which lie dormant within them, and under the right conditions, they will mature (and do so quickly) into adults possessing these powers. Unwittingly, the documentary depicted what Dewey calls the "negative" sense of capacity or potentiality—a state in which the potentialities lie "dormant," waiting for the appropriate external conditions that will allow them to blossom into "something different," namely, the adult powers that constitute the terminus of growth.

However, seen from the point of view of the chicks, this capacity to grow is a positive thing; their potentiality should be seen as a "power," "potency" or "force." In lucid prose Dewey points out that our "tendency to take immaturity as mere lack, and growth as something which fills up the gap between the immature and the mature," is a result of us treating immaturity "simply as a privation because we are measuring it by adulthood as a fixed standard." (Here it is worth drawing attention to the work of the great developmental psychologist Jean Piaget, who also focused on children as functioning organisms, and what they were able to achieve—and what they were not able to achieve—with their present capacities.) What Dewey is doing in these opening paragraphs is softening up the reader for the denouement that comes later: the process of growth (especially in humans, if not in pelicans) *has no fixed external ends*. But I am jumping the gun!

To lead us further down the path toward this conclusion, Dewey next makes two somewhat related points about prolonged infancy and flexibility in development of humans. He argues that the extremely prolonged immaturity of human youngsters is compensated for by their possession of "social gifts." For example, newly hatched turtles can immediately walk (or rather, waddle) down to the ocean and then are able to swim away—hundreds of them all at once, all seemingly acting independently—and pelican chicks take only a matter of weeks to become adults or at least adolescents, whereas it takes the human infant the better part of a year just to become a "toddler." Two paragraphs before the start of the second section of the chapter, Dewey writes that this "original specialized power of adjustment" possessed by many animal species "secures immediate efficiency, but, like a railway ticket, it is good for one route only." In short, the animal "is limited by the relative perfection of its original endowment." On the other hand, human infants, Dewey says in subsection 1 of the first part of chapter 4, "can get along with physical incapacity just because of their social capacity. . . . Children are gifted with an equipment of the first order for social intercourse." This dependence of the infant on others in the social group is not a sign of weakness, but rather is an indicator of that vital human feature—social interdependence—and, crucially, it allows the infant time to practice skills that are fully developed (or nearly so) in the newborns of other species, practice that contributes to later flexibility in the use of these powers.

Why, one might ask, is Dewey taking such pains to stress the long period of dependence of the human infant? Because he wants to lead us to the conclusion that—in contrast to other animals in which the process of growth has a fixed and inflexible end or goal—in humans there is no such built-in end. And to make this case Dewey believes it is necessary to stress the flexible nature of the skills or abilities that the child develops and masters, for it is this flexibility that opens the "possibility of continuing progress." And so ends the first section of the chapter.

Before moving further into the chapter, however, it is worth drawing attention to another of those short brilliant passages that are sprinkled throughout the book. Right at the end of the first subsection of the first part of chapter 4, Dewey observes that sometimes an individual does not recognize the importance of social interdependence, and he becomes "so insensitive to his relations to others as to develop an illusion of being really able to stand and act alone—an unnamed form of insanity which is responsible for a large part of the remediable suffering of the world." To which one can say, "Amen!"

The chapter's second section is devoted to discussing habits, toward which Dewey has an interesting—and largely positive—attitude. At first sight, this might strike many readers as odd, for habits have a poor reputation and are often viewed as the antithesis of liberating. (My habit of eating chocolate and drinking black coffee while grading student papers is a case in point.) Dewey, however, has in mind intelligent habits, which originate from what we have learned from previous experience; and he warns (near the end of the section) that habits that have become "routine" and "unthinking," and that are dissociated from intelligence, "enslave" us and have a "fixed hold upon us" (and thus I have come to the realization that I am enslaved by my habit of consuming caffeine and chocolate). But intelligent habits, on the other hand, are dispositions to act in certain ways, and they result in "an increase in ease, economy, and efficiency of action." And, of course, such habits are revisable in light of new experience. Consider, for example, the habits associated with driving a car—these save the driver from a great deal of constant effort and concentration, but they are enslaving or unintelligent if they are not open to improvement in light of experience. (I recall vividly the first time my car went into a serious skid; the incident caused me to reflect on and change some of my driving habits; such flexibility, however, is not found with the habits of many other animal species.) One other noteworthy point Dewey makes about habits is that when conceptualized as habituation, they are relatively passive things that serve to adjust us to the environment; but when seen from the perspective he is canvassing, they are "quite as much adaptation *of* the environment to our own activities as of our activities to the environment." The "civilized man," he writes, "has habits which transform the environment."

Here, and indeed throughout the chapter (and for that matter the entire book), Dewey's attachment to the theory of evolution is lying just beneath the surface—a matter that he alerted us to in his preface. Recall that, following William James, Dewey regarded the mind (the ability to think) as an adaptive feature we acquired in the course of evolution, an adaptation that had the function of contributing to our survival in the struggle for existence. This capacity allows us to formulate and then test ideas, plans of action and hypotheses, about how to resolve the "problematic situations" in which we find ourselves; and it also allows us to revise these ideas and plans in light of experience. In short, we have survived as a species largely by virtue of the fact that we have intelligent and therefore flexible and revisable habits or dispositions or modes of behavior. Writing about our capacity to formulate ideas, in chapter 4 of *The School and Society*, Dewey said that before the work of James, "the possibility of their origin in and from the needs of action was ignored," but now we see that the human capacity to formulate and test ideas "can have but one essential function—the function of defining the direction which our activity, immediate or remote, can take." (It should be noted that Dewey is doing a rare thing here—he is directly quoting an author, in this case, of course, William James himself.)

We have now arrived at what probably is the most famous part of chapter 4, if not the whole book. For in section 3, Dewey turns to the "educational bearings" of his preceding discussion, and in the opening six paragraphs or so, there are several passages that frequently have been quoted and that have, indeed, become slogans for many educators in the progressive movement. A few of these will be sufficient to frame our discussion. Dewey starts by asserting that his conclusions about growth, if justified, "carry with them . . . definite educational conclusions," and then he writes:

> Our net conclusion is that life is development, and that developing, growing, is life. Translated into its educational equivalents that means *(i)* that the educational process has no end beyond itself; it is its own end; and that *(ii)* the educational process is one of constant reorganizing, reconstructing, transforming.

A mistake often made in the past, he adds a little later, has been that "growth is regarded as *having* an end, instead of *being* an end" ("end," of course, in the sense of "goal" or "ultimate direction"). Finally, a paragraph and a half later he famously remarks:

> Since in reality there is nothing to which growth is relative save more growth, there is nothing to which education is subordinate save more education.

There is much room here for critical analysis; but to allay the feeling of some readers that the following discussion is mere "sour grapes," I should disclose that I am one among the many who—over the years—have found these passages to be sources of great inspiration.

The first comment focuses on Dewey's style of argumentation, which is reminiscent of his invalid use of "thus" in chapter 2, and which is also a style that he very frequently adopts. (It might be too unkind to point out that his arguing in this mode is almost an inflexible habit.) The issue is this: Often after discussing some theoretical or philosophical position—which he might be advocating, or rejecting as deficient in some way—Dewey asserts that there are what he variously calls "educational correlates," "educational morals," "educational equivalents," or "educational conclusions" that these positions "carry with them." The trouble is that they do not "carry" these conclusions or morals with them at all! For when propositions are being used in arguments about education—propositions that are about the body-mind problem in philosophy, or about flexibility in growth of habits, and so forth—and when these make no mention of education, then *something else, some other premise or set of premises*, is required to link the original proposition to education. And furthermore, different links may lead to different "educational morals" being drawn. (In my first book, published many decades ago in a different millennium—and on a different continent!—I showed that the same theoretical statement from Piaget's developmental theory in psychology could be linked to quite opposing educational morals or correlates or conclusions, depending on what other intermediary premises were used.)

In light of this discussion, consider the first of the block quotations above. Even if it is true that "life is development," it does not validly follow that "development is life." (Consider: even if it is true that, as the saying goes, "ignorance is bliss," it does not follow that "bliss is ignorance," for it can be many other things as well.) Nor, moreover, does it follow from this statement about life that "the educational process is its own end"; in other words, the argument "life is development, and therefore education is its own end" is invalid—indeed it appears to be a classic non sequitur. And, alas, the same can be said of "since in reality there is nothing to which growth is relative save more growth, there is nothing to which education is subordinate save more education." (There is another issue here that I will not pursue in depth; namely, Dewey seems to be mistaken about growth. In nature there are many organisms that stop growing when they reach maturity—a fact known to many avid gardeners who plant specific shrubs because they will remain small and not continue to grow like Jack's beanstalk.)

Dewey may, or may not, have been serious in using this invalid form of argumentation, but it has always seemed to me that there is a way of reading him that resolves the problem. Maybe he was not intent on crafting a waterproof argument at all, but rather was offering up a *vision*. Great philosophers, social theorists, and reformers, among others, often do produce arguments to support the positions they hold; but some of their work can also be regarded as presenting a challenge to the reader, a challenge along the following lines: "Look at the world from the perspective I have described—through the lens that I have crafted—and you will have a vision that previously was hidden from you. You will see phenomena afresh." Applying this to Dewey, then, we can read him as saying roughly this: Think of education as being a type of growth, and you will see that it is an ongoing process. A person who is growing in knowledge and understanding does not say, "Now I am educated, and so I can stop! I have read a play by Shakespeare, I know some basic science, I know the basic precepts of the world's great religions, I have browsed through a few dialogues by Plato, I can hum the opening of Beethoven's 'Fifth.' . . . . That's enough—I can take the rest of my life off." A truly educated person keeps inquiring, growing in knowledge, appreciation, and understanding.

It might be objected here that it is common to hear remarks like "Denis was educated at the University of Melbourne," which implies he underwent a finite process that constituted his education. The reply Dewey would give—and he would be joined by many of our contemporary analytic philosophers of education—is that in taking this tack the common mistake is being made of confusing *schooling* with education. Thus it would be more accurate to say that Denis's formal schooling was completed at the University of Melbourne, but not his education!

Reading Dewey in the way I have suggested highlights a further challenge to us: If education is, indeed, a never-ending process of growth in knowledge and understanding, how can educators (who are working in an institution such as a school or university) not only contribute to this growth of their students but perhaps even more importantly make it likely that they will continue to grow after they have moved on? Quite a challenge, but one that Dewey recognizes a couple of paragraphs before his summary:

> It is a commonplace to say that education should not cease when one leaves school. The point of this commonplace is that the purpose of school education is to insure that education should not cease when one leaves school. . . . Education means the enterprise of supplying the conditions which insure growth, or adequacy of life, irrespective of age.

It is time to turn to other comments about Dewey's discussion of growth and education. The first of these concerns a difficulty about the direction of growth. In Dewey's view, just as a skilled gardener will take note of the native capacities and inclinations of the plant under cultivation, and will help these come to fruition, so the educator will foster the development of the native capacities of the young learner, allowing these to blossom forth in all directions. But as with plants, so with children; growth can (and does) take place in directions that are judged to be undesirable by gardeners and educators. Dewey places no strictures on gardeners, who are free to impose their tastes and who can slash and burn and prune and graft at will; but he has insisted that educators not impose their adult ends on growing children. Educators can guide and stimulate—but this seems to beg the question, "stimulate in what direction?" Dewey's answer—"in the direction of further growth"—is not a sufficient guide, for it does not rule out growth in antisocial directions. But rule it out he must.

Here in D&E there are glimmers that Dewey is aware of the dilemma that faces him (roughly, how to encourage growth in certain directions without directing it); this is the point, one might suppose, of the long extract he quotes from Emerson at the end of the chapter. The interested and impatient reader might wish to jump ahead in this companion, to the final chapter where this issue will reappear; but for those who resist this temptation, it can be said that Dewey does not abandon his original position but tries to deal with the problem by refining and expanding it. But it cannot be said that he solves the problem in 1916; and as this problem would not go away, Dewey needed to return to it, which he did about two decades later in chapter 3 of his *Experience and Education* (1938). And he now is crystal clear about the nature of the problem, and illustrates it with an example that has stimulated much discussion down the years:

> That a man may grow in efficiency as a burglar, as a gangster, or as a corrupt politician, cannot be doubted. But from the standpoint of growth as education and education as growth the question is whether growth in this direction promotes or retards growth in general. . . . Does it set up conditions that shut off the person who has grown in this particular direction from the occasions, stimuli, and opportunities for continuing growth in new directions?

As mentioned, our attention will be drawn once again to the burglar and his growth when we arrive at the discussion of "theories of morals" in the final chapter of D&E.

My third and final major comment is about Dewey's position that development or growth has no end or goal beyond itself, and that the same can be said of education. Considerable light is shed on Dewey here when it is recognized that there are significant parallels—that he does not alert the reader to—between his use of "growth" and "education" and a concept dating back to the writings of Kant in the late eighteenth century and then Hegel in the early nineteenth century, namely, *Bildung*. Although it has no direct equivalent in English, and although its meaning has changed a little over the centuries (as has the meaning of many terms), it is generally agreed that a fair translation of this word is "self-development" or better still "self-formation," especially in the spiritual or at least the nonphysical domains. Here is a summary of the account of the term given by Hans-Georg Gadamer, perhaps the leading German philosopher of the last part of the twentieth century:

> Kant . . . speaks of "cultivating" a capacity (or "natural talent"), which as such is an act of freedom by the acting subject. Thus among duties to oneself he mentions not letting one's talents rust. . . . When Hegel takes up the same Kantian idea of duties to oneself, he already speaks of *Sichbildung* (educating or cultivating oneself) and *Bildung*.

A paragraph later Gadamer adds these enlightening words:

> The result of *Bildung* is not achieved in the manner of a technical construction, but grows out of an inner process of formation and cultivation, and therefore constantly remains in a state of continual *Bildung*. It is not accidental that in this respect the word *Bildung* resembles the Greek *physis*. *Like nature, Bildung has no goals outside itself.* (*Truth and Method*, 2nd rev. ed. [1993], pp. 10–11; italics added)

The parallel between the Germanic philosophical tradition's use of *Bildung* and Dewey's use of *growth* in educational contexts is startling and cannot be due to mere coincidence. For the fact is that Dewey's philosophical education took place in this very tradition—for example, he obtained his doctorate at Johns Hopkins under scholars who themselves had studied in Germany, and his first books and journal articles were on Hegelian and Kantian themes. Furthermore, later in life he wrote that "acquaintance with Hegel has left a permanent deposit in my thinking." And he added: "The form, the schematism, of his system now seems to me artificial to the last degree. But in the content of his ideas there is often an extraordinary depth" ("From Absolutism to Experimentalism" [1930], p. 21).

By the time D&E was written Dewey was well into his fifties, and the influence of Hegel lay (partially) hidden beneath the surface of his writings—due in large part to the work of William James, work that persuaded Dewey that the positions he had defended in his first forty or so years by using Hegelian arguments could be defended less artificially using naturalistic, evolutionary arguments. In the same essay where he had acknowledged the influence of Hegel, he wrote of James: "As far as I can discover one specifiable philosophic factor which entered into my thinking so as to give it a new direction and quality, it is this one." According to this analysis, then, Dewey had taken the concept of *Bildung* and naturalized or "biologized" it—instead of a conception of self-formation driven by neo-Kantian or neo-Hegelian metaphysics, it became the concept of *growth* driven by late nineteenth-century evolutionary biology. And like *Bildung*, this conception of growth has no end outside itself; it is its own end.

Finally, I cannot resist the temptation to mention Horne's bizarre comment (there is no other way of describing it) that appears in his discussion of Dewey's theory of growth. He writes:

> In discussing the unending character of growth, rejecting the static ideal of "ungrowth," it would be a reasonable inquiry at this point to ask whether the death of the human individual means the cessation of his growth. A cemetery at the end of life, if that is all, seems static "ungrowth" indeed. It is not enough to reply that society goes on, though the individual ceases to be, for some astronomers tell us that death awaits human society too. What then happens to the organic ideal of growth, unless there be immortal progress? (p. 42)

Bizarre indeed—but on the other hand, if you believe (as Horne did) that there is a realm of reality that transcends the natural world, and that is beyond or above the limits of time and space, an account of growth that neglects this is truly bizarre.

5

Preparation, Unfolding, and Formal Discipline

The aim of this chapter is straightforward—to shore up support for Dewey's conception of the "educative process" as being a "continuous process of growth" by showing the defects of the positions that are its chief rivals. Nevertheless it is a very difficult chapter for the contemporary reader to follow in all its detail, for among other things, Dewey discusses—and disposes of—three philosopher-theorists with whom some will not be familiar, namely, Froebel, Hegel, and Locke; and he does this in a mere dozen pages or so. It is a heroic effort, given the complexity of their thought. It is important therefore not to lose sight of the forest because of the trees; so the reader is cautioned to keep in mind the three rival positions about education as growth that Dewey is determined to undermine—namely, that education is a process of preparation, that it is a process of unfolding, and that it is a process of training the inborn faculties by exercising them ("formal discipline").

In light of his discussion in earlier chapters, Dewey's position with respect to preparation comes as no surprise. Preparation is directed toward adult life, and thus implies "the negative and privative character of growth already criticized." In a brilliant turn of phrase Dewey says that from this perspective children "are looked upon as candidates; they are placed on the waiting list." He wastes no time in turning to, as he puts it in one of his commonly used formulations, "the evil consequences that flow" from this view of education. (I merely will note in passing the point made earlier, that these consequences are not tight "logical consequences.") The first of the three consequences he points to is that, as children live in the present (as he puts it elsewhere, they are alive at the time they are alive and not at some other time), and as the future for which they are being prepared is a long way off, there is a severe loss of motivation to learn; and second, there is a concomitant tendency to "postpone opportunities," and this can lead to "shilly-shallying." Finally, because the future has "no stimulating and directing power when severed from the possibilities of the present," the preparation approach must rely on "adventitious motives" such as pleasure and pain to attempt to drive the learner. Dewey goes on to stress that of course education should prepare for the future, but what is at issue is how this is done. His position is that when every energy is "bent to making the present experience as rich and significant as possible" then—because the present merges into the future—the future is taken care of.

Dewey next turns his attention to a closely related theory that also is a defective theory of growth, namely, that education is a process of unfolding—the unfolding or development of "latent powers" toward a definite and preset goal. This certainly is not what he means by growing, which he regards as a continuous process with no fixed end point.

It is worth discussing "unfolding" in a little more detail. Perhaps the classic example in biology is the germination of a bean seed. After it is planted, the seed takes in water and swells until the outer cover bursts. Then, lo! two small projections fold out from within the seed. One of these (the radicle) grows downward and becomes the root, and the other (the hypocotyl), bearing the remnant of the seed, grows upward to become the stem with two nascent leaves. It is all as Dewey describes: the power to develop root and stem and leaves is within the seed; given the right conditions, these unfold and grow to attain their fixed, preordained end points or goals.

But a problem arises: It is fairly obvious what is "inborn" in a germinating bean seed, but it is not at all obvious in the case of young human beings. As should by now be clear, Dewey rejects this account of growth as a model for the development of human youngsters. And so the difficult discussion in chapter 5 comes about—Dewey focuses on two different philosophical accounts of the nature of what it is that is inborn and then unfolds in the course of human development. One of these accounts comes from Friedrich Froebel (1782–1852), the founder of the kindergarten movement who had an interest in the philosophical idealist tradition, and the other was taken from the great idealist philosopher G. W. F. Hegel (1770–1831). Dewey selects these two for discussion because they represent different tendencies within idealism, and of course both their positions are deficient!

Both men accepted the core belief of Absolute Idealism that all that happens within the physical sphere, including the historical trajectory of human affairs, is a result of a spiritual or metaphysical entity or principle—the Absolute—struggling to make itself manifest. According to Dewey's account, Froebel believed that the Absolute was immanent within all humans, and when it was roused from its "sleep" (as Dewey phrases it), it directed our development, and indeed the entire trajectory of our lives. The use of symbols was the means by which the Absolute within us could be awakened. Here an analogy—imperfect as it is—might serve to make this more reasonable to the nonidealist mind. It might be supposed that within many humans there is an inborn "drive" toward creativity, a drive that constantly struggles to make itself manifest. Under the right stimulating conditions (at the hands of a gifted arts teacher, for example), this creative ability will unfold and display itself. So it is, according to Froebel, with the Absolute within us.

What, then, is the educational defect Dewey sees here? Simply that this theory places the educational decisions (for example, about what symbolism to present to children and how to do so) outside the developing child and in the hands of adults, who have in mind the "completed product" and not the ongoing open process of development.

Hegel, on the other hand, regarded the Absolute as being immanent in human institutions whose development over time reflected its self-development; thus the social institutions (which include "language, government, art, religion") that exist at any time reflect the stage of development of the Absolute at that period. As Dewey puts it in the second-to-last paragraph of section 2, according to Hegel,

> against institutions as they are, individuals have no spiritual rights; personal development, and nurture, consist in obedient assimilation of the spirit of existing institutions. Conformity, not transformation, is the essence of education.

So, from this perspective, what unfolds during the process of individual development are faculties that equip the individual for living in harmony with the contemporary social institutions. An exception is the development from time to time of those few "heroes" whose life attainments push the development of the Absolute onward and upward. It is clear that this Hegelian theory, like the Froebelian, places control of the process of child development in factors (institutions) external to the child. "In its notion of a complete and all-inclusive end of development, the Hegelian theory swallowed up concrete individualities," Dewey wrote at the end of section 2. And so we arrive at section 3.

What Dewey critiques here is the theory that educational growth consists in the "training of faculties." According to this view, just as a pelican chick has within it the nascent ability to fly, an ability that needs to be sharpened with (physical) exercise—such things as flapping of the wings, and "pushing off" with the legs—so too does a human youngster arrive in the world with undeveloped physical, but crucially also cognitive, abilities or faculties that need to be fostered through exercise. When they are fully developed, these abilities or faculties could be used in a wide variety of situations. It is the aim of education, according to this view, to provide the relevant training, and the best material to use for this is formal or abstract in nature—for instance, classical languages and mathematics.

Dewey correctly identifies the empiricist philosophy of John Locke (1632–1704) as being the historical linchpin of this theory. For Locke famously argued that at birth the human infant's mind is empty—it is a blank slate (a "tabula rasa") or an "empty cabinet." How, then, does it come to be "furnished" with content, with ideas? Locke answered this question with one word: the mind is furnished by way of *experience*. But, crucially, although at birth the mind has no content, it comes already equipped with powers or faculties. (Some later theorists, it can be noted in passing, were bold enough to hold that these faculties also are not inborn but originate in experience; and there was much debate about the precise number and identities of these faculties.)

There is an analogy that might be helpful here in clarifying the Lockean position: Consider a tablet or smartphone. Right out of the box these marvels of contemporary technology are without contents—they do not have the phone numbers or e-mail addresses of one's friends, and they do not have a list of one's favorite movies, let alone downloaded copies of them. But they do have the capacity (or faculties or abilities) to store such things, and to send e-mails and perform calculations, and to format documents, and to make playlists—for these abilities were "wired in" by the designers of these technological wonders. But in one respect the analogy breaks down; the abilities of the tablet or smartphone do not get strengthened through use, whereas (according to the theory Dewey was attacking) the inborn human faculties do improve with exercise.

The theory that mental capacities or faculties can be strengthened through exercise (just as the muscles of an athlete can be strengthened by way of training) has persisted, indeed flourished, down through the centuries. I can recall falling victim to the theory myself in my early high school years. By some mysterious process I had been placed in a Latin class, and on the very first day, the teacher—who was overbearing enough to have been a Roman himself—told us that because "any fool can learn material that is interesting," he would make no effort to make Latin appealing. The value of the course, he insisted, would come from the development of certain mental abilities that would flow from our hours of practice—concentrating on, and remembering, material that was dull! Needless to say, I did not earn an A in this class; and no doubt the deficiency in my faculties of concentration and memory can be traced back to my lack of wholehearted participation in this unholy regimen of exercise. Many years later I discovered that my teacher had been tapping into a traditional defense for Latin being on the curriculum; as the practical benefits of mastery of it declined (after all, there were, even then, no countries on Earth where Latin was the native language—with the dubious exception of the Vatican state), its value as a "formal," abstract discipline that could train the faculties of memory, concentration, and so on, was accentuated. And of great significance was the associated belief that these newly enhanced or strengthened faculties could then be used in quite different contexts—a doctrine known as "transfer of learning." Unfortunately for the fortunes of the classical languages, the empirical evidence that was starting to accumulate did not support either of these claims! Coincidentally, some of the key studies that undermined the traditional doctrine of transfer were carried out by William James and Dewey's colleague E. L. Thorndike.

Dewey does not attack either of these dubious claims by citing the relevant research studies, with which he must have been quite familiar, but instead he offers a different and interesting line of criticism; namely, faculties as conceptualized in the tradition he is examining do not exist at all. "There are no such ready-made powers waiting to be exercised and thereby trained," he writes. His argument justifying this important criticism is rather mysterious unless one is acquainted with some history (although it must be admitted that when all is said and done some of the mystery will remain).

By the late nineteenth century, a central place in psychology was accorded to the "reflex arc," wherein a stimulus received by a sensory receptor produced a signal that was conducted to (and through) some part of the central nervous system, such as the spinal chord, and without requiring conscious guidance was then conducted by a motor nerve out to a muscular system where it induced an automatic response or reaction. A prime example of an action explained by this reflex arc is the automatic, involuntary, and almost instantaneous withdrawing of an infant's hand when it has grasped a hot object. Many researchers and theorists regarded the reflex arc as being the basic "unit" of animal and human nervous systems—in short, psychologically animals (including us) are very complex bundles of reflexes. In 1896 Dewey published an extremely influential paper (which was the origin of what became known as the school of functional psychology) in which he argued that the linear pattern attributed to a reflex arc, stimulus→central nervous system→response, was mistaken, and the reflex had to be reconceptualized as a coordination or *circuit*. (This is one of those occasions referred to in my introduction when Dewey is advocating a new and unfamiliar way of looking at or conceptualizing some situation—a way we readers a century or more later may have to struggle to fully understand.)

One way to make Dewey's position comprehensible to a reader in the twenty-first century is to start with his insight that the reflex arc theory is not a valid description of the relevant phenomena but rather a theoretical account or interpretation imposed on them. In the actual process, Dewey insists, "there is nothing which can be set off as stimulus, nothing which reacts, nothing which is response. There is just a change in the system of tensions." Recall the example of the baby's hand. Dewey's point is that it is not an accurate description to say that the baby is reacting to the stimulus of the hot object. The baby does not know what an object is, or what heat is, so he or she cannot be reacting to, or learning to avoid on subsequent occasions, the stimulus of the hot object. The baby merely grasps a thing and instantaneously drops it and starts to cry in pain. This sequence of events occurs to the whole baby, and not to an isolated hand remotely connected to some muscles in its arm. It is only afterward, and perhaps after several other episodes that vary slightly in detail, that there is a glimmer that the thing grasped is an object, that it is hot, and that grasping it leads to pain and the dropping of the object. It is only then, perhaps, that the hot poker becomes a "stimulus." Some of Dewey's language is almost poetic, but it hardly is helpful to the contemporary reader:

> What we have is a circuit, not an arc or broken segment of a circle. This circuit is more truly termed organic than reflex, because the motor response determines the stimulus, just as truly as sensory stimulus determines movement. Indeed, the movement is only for the sake of determining the stimulus, of fixing what kind of stimulus it is, or interpreting it. ("The Reflex Arc Concept in Psychology" [1896])

Dewey's paper has four "take-home" messages: First, the stimulus is only identifiable *as* a stimulus having such-and-such a nature in light of the response that had been elicited—in short, the response determines the stimulus at the same time that the stimulus determines the response. Second, the traditional account of the reflex arc ignores the fact that the response makes some change to the environment, setting, or situation in which this reflex circuit is operating (human action always makes some change to the environment), and thus the nature of subsequent stimulus-and-response circuits is affected. Third, the traditional reflex arc theory ignores the fact that the whole organism, and indeed the organism plus the environment, is involved in a so-called reflex action (eyes, neck and leg muscles, for example, are involved as much as the hand in the case of grasping a hot object). And fourth, the point we started with, namely, the language of the reflex arc account—which he says is a theory with a "disjointed character"—is not valid as a description of what happens but is an interpretation.

Returning to chapter 5 of D&E, it now can be seen that Dewey adopts a stance toward faculties that parallels the one he had adopted to the reflex arc. Faculty psychology did not offer a valid description of the relevant phenomena but rather put forward a theory or interpretation. The notion that there are faculties is "purely mythological"; there are no "ready-made powers waiting to be exercised and thereby trained"; instead there are a "great number of original native tendencies" that are of "an indefinite variety, interweaving with one another in all kinds of subtle ways." These "tendencies" guide our interaction with the environment and foster our "utilization" of it. Those "diffuse responses" that prove to be ineffective at this task are gradually eliminated; those that survive get refined with further experience, and—although Dewey does not specifically say this—one might suppose that these get identified, mistakenly, as "faculties." Dewey does point out that this whole process has been misidentified as "training by exercise." As he puts it at the beginning of subsection 2 of this section on faculties,

> The *training* of our original impulsive activities is not a refinement and perfecting achieved by "exercise" as one might strengthen a muscle by practice. It consists rather . . . in *selecting* from the diffused responses which are evoked at a given time those which are especially adapted to the *utilization* of the stimulus.

As part of this "training" via selection of responses, the youngster learns to *coordinate* the many "different factors" involved in making a response.

Dewey makes one further, related criticism of faculty psychology: the so-called faculties that are trained by formal discipline have been artificially divorced from subject matter. He is forthright:

> There is no such thing as an ability to see or hear or remember in general; there is only the ability to see or hear or remember *something*. To talk about training a power, mental or physical, in general, apart from the subject matter involved in its exercise, is nonsense.

For example, it is far, far easier for a person who knows some chemistry to remember complex chemical equations than it is for a scientific ignoramus (who might find the task impossible);

yet this chemist will fare dismally at remembering abstract Latin grammar unless he or she also has some background in the classics.

Finally, Dewey points out that we might develop one narrow, specific skill by subjecting a student to a regimen of repetition of a "monotonously uniform exercise," but the skill will be limited to this one specific setting and does not "ramify" (transfer) into other fields. And close to the end of the chapter, Dewey has a passage that could have been directed at my high school Latin teacher: Dewey is focusing here on how to educate a person to become an effective member of a social group such as chemists or botanists, and he points out that this must involve meaningful interaction with a body of subject matter and also interaction with other members of this social group,

> otherwise we might as well set the pupil to observing carefully cracks on the wall and set him to memorizing meaningless lists of words in an unknown tongue—which is about what we do in fact when we give way to the doctrine of formal discipline.

In response to which, all I can say is QED.

6

Education as Conservative and Progressive

The preceding couple of chapters discussed education as growth, and the focus was on growth of faculties or powers or abilities. This chapter shifts our attention to education as growth in content or ideas, a focus that was presaged in the final portion of chapter 5. The going here is not nearly as rough as it was previously.

The chapter opens clearly enough with a discussion of "education as formation," which Dewey says is not a process of unfolding "from within," nor is it the development of faculties "resident in mind itself"; rather, it is formation of the mind by instruction, that is, a "building into the mind" from outside. In terms of the illustration of the tablet and smartphone used in the previous chapter, whereas the theorists interested in "unfolding" and the like were focused on the inborn powers of the device, Herbart and his followers were interested in how the contents of the device were fed into it, with how it came to be "furnished" with ideas. For them, mind *was* the contents—no ideas, no mind! Dewey does not give much detail about Herbart himself, probably because in 1916 Herbart was still quite a well-known and influential thinker; but background is certainly required for most twenty-first-century readers.

Johann Friedrich Herbart (1776–1841) was a German philosopher who also wrote on education; at one time he held the chair in philosophy that had been occupied by Immanuel Kant. His educational theories became influential after his death, and in the mid-1890s educationists in the USA (including John Dewey) established the National Herbart Society; in 1901 this name was changed to the National Society for the Study of Education (NSSE)—under which the society flourished throughout the twentieth century.

The two aspects of Herbart's educational work that were particularly influential were his theory of mind and his theory of teaching (I recall receiving a lecture on this latter topic during my own teacher training—more than a century after Herbart's death). Stripped of philosophical refinement, his theory of mind held that the mind just was a collective made up of the ideas that had been received and retained from "outside" (via instruction or experience). To become an active part of this collective—which he called the "apperceptive mass"—new ideas being received needed to be compatible with, and connected in some way to, the ideas that were already present; in other words, the apperceptive mass determined what new ideas would be acquired, what would be rejected, and what would be filed away in the realm of the unconscious. I am tempted to remark here that all of this is now part of what many readers will regard as common sense, as all of us have had the experience of struggling to understand and remember ideas that were discordant with, or entirely disconnected from, those things we already knew. And it is part of common sense, too, to believe that we often understand the new in terms of the old.

The issue arises, of course, that given this view of mind, how can the learning of—the acquisition of—new material, new ideas, be facilitated? Here is where Herbart's theory of instruction and the famed "Herbartian steps" enter. The basic idea is that both the new ideas and the ones already in the mind need to be prepared so that their introduction to each other is successful, and guidance must be given about how to integrate the new with the currently existing. This process takes place in a number of steps, the first three of which are preparation, presentation, and association; these are followed by a step involving guiding the learner in generalizing the newly implanted idea. The fifth and final step is the application of the new idea so that it becomes a fully integrated part of the functioning mind. Over the years, I have visualized these five steps as being roughly analogous to what happens when a racing car engine is fitted with some new device to make it perform even better (as I am an ignoramus here, I cannot be more specific). The new part needs to be prepared so that it is likely to connect up properly; but the existing engine also needs preparation in the relevant spot so that it is able to accommodate the new item. The mechanic must insert the new part in the correct place, and then run the engine to see if the whole thing fires up. Finally, the car is taken out of the coddled environment of the garage and given an open-ended road test where it will face new conditions.

In chapter 6 Dewey expounds all of this and remarks that Herbart performed a service in bringing the process of teaching "into the sphere of conscious method." Then, in another of his striking turns of phrase, he damns Herbart with faint praise near the end of the chapter's first section:

> The theory represents the Schoolmaster come to his own. . . . The conception that the mind consists of what has been taught, and that the importance of what has been taught consists in its availability for further teaching, reflects the pedagogue's view of life.

Dewey seems to regard Herbart's approach as too mechanical and conservative, and lists the defects of the approach that neglect the essence of education, which is "vital energy seeking opportunity for effective exercise." But here there is an issue that the contemporary reader may find worthwhile to ponder: Is there still something important to be learned from Herbart? A century on from D&E, we live in an era with a plethora of abstract theories that an educated person needs to be acquainted with—ranging from economics to biochemistry and medicine, from cosmology and quantum physics to political theory and computer science. These fields are surely difficult for the unprepared mind to absorb, even partially—and might not the Herbartian method be a step in the right direction?

In section 2 of the chapter, Dewey turns to another theory about content that had been used quite widely to guide instructional policy. There are some hints in his earlier writings that Dewey tentatively accepted this theory, but in D&E he is clear that it was defective. His account is quite lucid, although once again he provides only a little background, apparently assuming that his readers in 1916 would understand. The theory of course is the theory of (cultural) recapitulation. Dewey disposes of it in a few paragraphs, but uses the opportunity to open up a wider topic about which he has some thought-provoking things to say—namely, what aspects of the past should play a role in education in and for the present? (He revisits this question again in chapter 16.)

The background that Dewey omitted is quite interesting in its own right. Perhaps the place to start is with the great German embryologist Karl Ernst von Baer (1792–1876). As the story goes, he had two embryos in specimen jars in his laboratory, the labels for which had gone missing; and he found that he could not tell if they were young lizards, birds, or mammals. For the fact is that, in the process of their development, embryos pass through "stages" in which they have the characteristics of their evolutionary forebears—or, more accurately, the characteristics of the embryos of some of their evolutionary forebears. Human embryos, for example, pass through a stage where they possess gill slits, comparable to those possessed by fish embryos as well as by fully developed fish. By the late nineteenth century some researchers were bold enough to claim that this fact could be used to make inferences to fill in gaps in the evolutionary record, for it was (as Ernst Haeckel and others claimed) a law of nature that "ontogeny recapitulates phylogeny," that is, the process of development to maturity of an individual recapitulates the stages of evolutionary development of that individual's group or species. It was this theory that Dewey rejected in 1916, writing that "without doubt" embryonic development preserves some of the traits of "lower forms of life," but crucially "in no respect is it a strict traversing of past stages." Yet it is interesting to note that the erroneous view persisted in popular culture. The best-selling book in the English language in the last decades of the twentieth century, after the Bible, was Dr. Benjamin Spock's *Baby and Child Care*—a book that is certain to be known by, if not the readers of this companion, many of their parents and grandparents. My own well-thumbed copy contains this wonderful passage that was at least a half century out of date:

> There's nothing in the world more fascinating than watching a child grow and develop. . . . Each child as he develops is retracing the whole history of mankind, physically and spiritually, step by step. The baby starts off in the womb as a single tiny cell, just the way the first living things appeared in the ocean. Weeks later, as he lies in the amniotic fluid in the womb, he has gills like a fish. Toward the end of his first year of life, when he learns to clamber to his feet, he's celebrating that period millions of years ago when man's ancestors got up off all fours. (2nd ed. [1963], p. 223)

According to some adherents of this theory in the late nineteenth century, recapitulation did not stop at birth. The youngster kept moving through stages that paralleled the great "cultural epochs" in the social evolution of the human species. This theory was used to provide curriculum guidance—the young learner should be exposed, in turn, to the great literary and other cultural works that were typical products of these epochs—because these (of course!) were compatible with the state of his or her mental development. Even today it is common to find children who are more familiar with the pharaohs, Egyptian art and myths, and Greek and Roman legends than they are with political leaders, major events, and literary works from our own age.

The final few pages of section 2 of the chapter are devoted to Dewey's rejection of the cultural epochs theory, but the discussion draws him into a broader and much more important topic—the nature of history education. He reiterates his main point several times in slightly different ways. In one key passage, which includes a striking phrase that I have taken the liberty to italicize, he writes:

> But an individual can live only in the present. The present is not just something which comes after the past; much less something produced by it. *It is what life is in leaving the past behind it.* The study of past [cultural] *products* will not help us understand the present, because the present is not due to the products, but to the life of which they were the products.

Dewey does not deny that the products of past epochs can be a great resource for the imagination, but unless they are connected to the demands of life in the present, they become a "refuge and asylum," and they allow individuals to "escape from the crudities of the present to live in its [the past's] imagined refinements."

This view of history—that past events, and cultural products of the past, are only suitable objects for study insofar as they "enter into the present"—has seemed to many critics of Dewey to represent the crass, utilitarian aspect of the philosophy of pragmatism. It may well do so, but that is a judgment for the reader to make. To put all the relevant cards on the table, however—and to risk damning Dewey even more—I should point out that Dewey is being a consistent pragmatist here. For pragmatism is a philosophy that, rather than turning to the past, is future oriented; for the pragmatists, the ability to think, to formulate and assess ideas, evolved in our species as an adaptive feature that has contributed to our survival in the evolutionary struggle for existence. Ideas (broadly construed to include factual and theoretical information) are, according to the pragmatists' account, tools or plans of action, the function of which is to intelligently guide our actions *now and in the future*. Thus, to be relevant in this task, the "heritage from the past" must be connected with "the demands and opportunities of the present." This is crass perhaps, but also, in its way, rather inspiring.

We have now arrived at section 3 of the chapter, and here Dewey turns from telling us what education is *not* to sketching what education *is*! If "education as growth" is not a matter of unfolding, formation, recapitulation, and so on, what is it? Dewey's answer is that it is growth in experience—not mere accumulation, but the continuing process of reorganization or reconstruction of experience to allow upgraded guidance to be exercised over the direction taken by subsequent experience. In a startling passage in the second paragraph of section 3, he writes:

> We thus reach a technical definition of education: It is that reconstruction or reorganization of experience which adds to the meaning of experience, and which increases ability to direct the course of subsequent experience.

The first unsettling thing about these lines is the appearance, once again, of "thus" where it is not warranted—the conclusion that follows this term is by no means a logical consequence of the preceding considerations that Dewey has offered. (To show that I am not prejudiced against this word, I should reveal that when personalized car license plates first became available, I applied for "THUS," but sadly it was already taken.) Second, the main surprise is that Dewey's "technical definition" is not a definition of education at all. (And, by the way, what does he mean by "technical" here?)

The problem is that Dewey's account does not capture the meaning of the term "education" as it is used in everyday discourse—as an analytic philosopher might put it, he has not given an accurate "reportive definition." When we say that someone is educated, it seems quite unlikely that we mean by this what Dewey suggests we mean! Now Dewey might, of course, be trying to stipulate a *new* meaning or usage for the word rather than clarifying its ordinary-language usage, but if this is the case, he should have made this intention clear, and he would have had to provide a much more detailed argument to show that this new meaning was better in various respects than the traditional one. This becomes clear if we compare Dewey's "definition" with the account given by two leaders of the analytic ("ordinary language") philosophy of education movement in the 1960s and 1970s, Richard Peters and Paul Hirst; their account comes much closer to capturing what the term means in standard English usage: " 'Education' suggests not only that what develops in someone is valuable but also that it involves the development of knowledge and understanding. Whatever else an educated person is, he is one who has some understanding of something. He is not just a person who has know-how or knack. There is also the suggestion that this understanding should not be too narrowly specialized" (*The Logic of Education* [1970], p. 19).

Whether consciously or not, Dewey was not providing us with a definition; in my interpretation he is issuing his readers a challenge along these lines: stop thinking of education in terms of understandings that a person has achieved in the past, and instead think of it as preparation to live more successfully—more fruitfully—in the future by using present intellectual resources to open up future possibilities. It is an important challenge, even without a "thus."

The second-to-last paragraph of the chapter, before the summary, makes a point that at first glance may seem somewhat mysterious, and which might therefore be bypassed. In contrast with the other conceptions of educational growth he has critiqued, the view Dewey is canvassing "identifies the end (the result) and the process." The point—an important one—can best be explained by way of an analogy. Suppose an educator has devised a program, the aim of which is to produce students who do not accept views that are thrust upon them by some authority figure, but who think for themselves. It would be paradoxical if this program consisted of a series of lectures instructing students not to accept things on authority, lectures that were meant to be accepted by the student on the authority of the lecturer! If the goal of independent thinking is indeed valuable, then perhaps this skill ought to be practiced in the program itself—in other words, the means in this case should also embody the values that are reflected in the ends or goals. Dewey is making the same point about education as reconstruction of experience to enable it to fruitfully guide or lead to future experience. This is a goal, but the same value should infuse the educational process in the present!

7

The Democratic Conception in Education

Education takes place within a social group or society, a fact that up until this chapter Dewey has only acknowledged in passing. Here he launches into a full-fledged discussion, writing that "education is a social function, securing direction and development in the immature through their participation in the life of the group to which they belong." Hence education will vary with the "quality of life" that exists within these social groups.

In section 1 Dewey reminds the reader that there is an "endless variety" of types of "human association," with larger groups containing within them an assortment of smaller ones. An individual, of course, may belong to a number of groups. Dewey also makes clear that he counts among social groups such things as "men banded together in a criminal conspiracy" and "political machines held together by the interest of plunder"; although these are "opposed to the interests of other groups," they are societies nonetheless, for each has "something of the praiseworthy qualities of 'Society' which hold it together." These preliminary matters take three paragraphs, and by the time Dewey starts the fourth he is face-to-face with the $64,000 question—can he satisfy the "need for a measure for the worth of any given mode of social life"? He must to do this, because he wants to discuss education in a worthy society rather than an unworthy one. So then, why is a gang of thieves less worthy than, say, a farmers' collaborative; and why is a democratic polity of higher quality than a dictatorship or an oligarchy?

Once again Dewey's pragmatism comes into play here, and it prevents him from giving the most obvious answer. He cannot argue along the following lines: Stealing is evil, and farming is good and hence is of higher quality or value; and a democracy is better than a dictatorship because it is based on human equality and this is good or valuable in itself. Why not? Because pragmatists like Dewey do not believe in appealing to a transcendental realm of values or metaphysical "goods," for this represents an attempt to escape from the realities (and problems) of this world by seeking answers, or principles that can serve as guides, in a metaphysical realm that is outside (or transcends) the only world we can directly experience. In chapter 25 of D&E, Dewey writes of the "flight to some transcendental realm" as ending badly "in a division between things of this world as mere appearances and an inaccessible essence of reality." Pragmatists believe that our capacity to think evolved to aid us in living in—and facing the problems in—*this actual world*, and not in an *inaccessible transcendental* one. (A fuller and quite lucid criticism of transcendentalism can be found in *Reconstruction in Philosophy*.) In short, Dewey needs to find some naturalistic criterion (or criteria) that he can use to determine the "worth" of a social group ("naturalistic" meaning here something observable or detectable within the actual world that we inhabit).

Presumably after analyzing the features of a variety of social groups "which actually exist," and avoiding thinking about "ideal societies," Dewey reaches the conclusion that real groups vary along two crucial dimensions, and from this insight his "measure for the worth of any given mode of social life" emerges:

> Now in any social group whatever, even in a gang of thieves, we find some interest held in common, and we find a certain amount of interaction and cooperative intercourse with other groups. From these two traits we derive our standard. How numerous and varied are the interests which are consciously shared? How full and free is the interplay with other forms of association?

According to Dewey's analysis, in a criminal band the internal and external ties are few in number; but the situation is different for a family group—and so the latter society is a more worthy one. QED. Dewey spends the next few pages spelling out the deleterious consequences that flow when one or other of these criteria is not satisfied.

Some readers might join me in being uneasy about all of this. It feels as if Dewey has performed a feat of legerdemain in order to reach the conclusion he desired from the outset. Why, for example, when societies have very many features, did he select the number of links to other societies as one of the two key factors? And why did he judge a society as more worthy than another if it had more links to external social groups when there have been many societies that have placed very high value on being cut off and shielded from external influences? Clearly Dewey holds the opposing value, so why does he not just say that it is better to be connected than to be insulated? Of course, when challenged in this way Dewey's reply (given at the start of the very long final paragraph of section 1.1) is that a society that is well connected to others provides more opportunities for its members to have stimulating experiences—but why is this a good thing (especially when such "outside" experiences can have devastating consequences)? And so it goes—values must enter the account at some stage. This, at least, is what enters the mind of a critic when reading Dewey. But for now I leave this perplexing issue for the reader to resolve.

Unease about the structure of Dewey's argument—if the reader harbors it—should not distract attention from Dewey's conclusion: he is holding up for emulation the "open society" as opposed to the "closed society" (to use Karl Popper's later expressions), and an open society is a *democratic* one. In section 2 of the chapter, he spells out the "democratic ideal" and why this form of society must be committed to the education of all its members. "The devotion of democracy to education is a familiar fact," he writes, and the superficial explanation of this is that in a democracy all members of the electorate need to be educated so that they can vote wisely (the mantra is that because ordinary citizens are enfranchised, "we must educate our masters"). But there is a deeper reason, Dewey argues, that has its origin in the nature of democracy itself:

> A democracy is more than a form of government; it is primarily a mode of associated living, of conjoint communicated experience. The extension in space of the number of individuals who participate in an interest so that each has to refer his own action to that of others, and to consider the action of others to give point and direction to his own, is equivalent to the breaking down of those barriers of class, race, and national territory which kept men from perceiving the full import of their activity. These more numerous and more varied points of contact . . . secure a liberation of powers.

Given this,

> a society which is mobile, which is full of channels for the distribution of a change occurring anywhere, must see to it that its members are educated to personal initiative and adaptability. Otherwise they will be overwhelmed by the changes in which they are caught.

And so, essentially, we have arrived back at the evolutionary account of mind: it evolved to give intelligent direction to our actions in a dangerous and ever-changing environment, a role for which—in the modern world—it needs to be educated so as to have command of the various intellectual and other tools that have been developed.

We now have reached section 3 of the chapter, and from this point on the discussion takes a new direction. Dewey turns to the past, to three philosophical traditions that have influenced educational thought. All three are associated with a noted thinker, and all have something valuable to say about the "social import" of education—although all three have deficiencies.

It is with relief that I remind the reader that it is not the role of a companion to present a précis, especially of such complex and voluminous bodies of work. Furthermore, there is no need because Dewey does a creditable job of exposition (although certainly a reader with some prior acquaintance with the three traditions will be at some advantage). But offering a very brief summary—a "take-home message"—might be helpful. In the republic envisioned by Plato, the governing class was a small group of men and women whose abilities and training had equipped them to contemplate the (metaphysical) "form of the good" and govern society in light of this. This republic would be perfectly just, for each citizen would be doing the work for which he or she was naturally equipped. Dewey thought there was much to be admired in this, but it was the next point that drew his criticism—Plato believed that there were various types of work, demanding quite different sets of skills, and that on this basis the citizens of the republic could be divided neatly into three classes. In Dewey's view, this seriously underestimated the range of interests and abilities possessed by every individual—"each individual constitutes his own class"—and this defect eventually would lead a society to stagnate. It is interesting to note that Karl Popper also thought the republic would stagnate (or worse) because it was a *closed* society (closed from input that could lead to improvement).

The thinkers in the second tradition Dewey discusses, including most notably Jean-Jacques Rousseau, were "acutely conscious of the evils of the social estate in which they found themselves. They attributed these evils to the limitations imposed upon the free powers of man." As the opening sentence of Rousseau's novel *Emile* put it, in prose that rings down through the centuries, "God makes all things good; man meddles with them and they become evil." Until society is reformed, education should be "in accord with nature," and indeed such an education would eventually lead to the reformation that was needed. Dewey pointed to a major weakness inherent in this approach to education: "The weakness of the theory on the constructive side became obvious. Merely to leave everything to nature was, after all, but to negate the very idea of education; it was to trust to the accidents of circumstance."

The third tradition Dewey discusses arose, he claims, when the first flush of enthusiasm for the freedom advocated by Rousseau and others waned. It was realized that the support of the state was required to institute any system of education. Especially in the eyes of German thinkers (of whom the most prominent was Hegel), education came to be seen as a state function, and eventually the focus became the education of the citizen rather than the education of the individual. Attempts were made to resolve the tension between these two goals; it was argued that the state had an "organic" nature, according to which "the individual in his isolation is nothing; only in and through an absorption of the aims and meaning of organized institutions does he attain true personality." Throughout this discussion Dewey is hiding a juicy little secret from his readers. Two decades earlier he had advocated this very same Hegelian position in his short but influential essay "My Pedagogic Creed" (1897). But here in D&E he was aware of the danger that educational institutions, in a state where such an ideology was dominant, would have to "submit to jealous state regulation and supervision all private educational enterprises." In short, education would become a tool of state domination over the individual.

8

Aims in Education

At first sight the topic of this chapter—aims in education—is a rather pedestrian one. But in fact Dewey's discussion is a treasure trove of important ideas. However, before setting out to explore these, I need to make two points about the overall strategy that he adopts here. First, it needs to be stressed that it is not Dewey's purpose in chapter 8 to advocate a number of specific aims, but rather he is doing what many philosophers do at or near the outset of a project—he undertakes a necessary preliminary task, namely, the *clarification or analysis of the key concept that is involved.* His discussion of some specific aims is contained in later chapters of D&E. Second, although it remains rather murky until the end of the chapter (where it also might not be clear enough to satisfy some readers), Dewey distinguishes between two types of aims: aims as "ends in view," on which he spends most of the chapter, and "general" or "ultimate" aims or ends.

Dewey's main analytic point about aims is as follows: "The aim as a foreseen end gives direction to the activity; it is not the idle view of a mere spectator, but influences the steps taken to reach the end." An aim, he stresses, is not something external to the educational process and to which this is "subordinate," but rather (like all ideas) it should operate *within* the educational process. However, the significance of this, and of the other points he makes throughout, might not at first be appreciated by the reader. So I will cover the territory using an example drawn from one of my own classroom adventures many years ago.

I was teaching a high school class of more than thirty teenagers who were in the nonacademic track—essentially they seemed to be killing time, waiting to reach the legal age when they could leave school behind them and enter the workforce. The course was General Science, a mix of elementary chemistry, physics, biology, and astronomy, and its overall aim—according to the state authority that had prescribed it—was to show how modern science could fruitfully illuminate the phenomena of daily life. This was a fairly broad "end in view," but evidently it had functioned to shape the content of the course (the "means" that were to be adopted in order to attain this goal). The topics that had been decided on were mandatory for all teachers in the state who were teaching at the appropriate level, but there was some freedom allowed with respect to the order in which they were tackled. Dewey might have been looking over my shoulder when he wrote in section 3.2:

> The vice of externally imposed ends has deep roots. Teachers receive them from superior authorities. . . . The teachers impose them upon children. As a first consequence, the intelligence of the teacher is not free; it is confined to receiving the aims laid down from above. Too rarely is the individual teacher so free from the dictation of authoritative supervisor, textbook on methods, prescribed course of study, etc., that he can let his mind come to close quarters with the pupil's mind and the subject matter.

Thus—dutiful teacher that I was—around midyear I reached the topic "temperature and its measurement: centigrade and Fahrenheit scales." The size of the class, the proclivity to misbehavior of some of its members, the fact that I was running behind schedule, and the topic itself (there had been an audible groan when I had foreshadowed, the end of the week before, what we would be doing next), all dictated (I thought) that I should cover the material as quickly as possible. Resolutely I pushed ahead with a series of what used to be called "chalk-and-talk" lessons. My goals, together with my appraisal of the prevailing conditions, certainly influenced my choice of content and the methods I used to teach it. In short, all seemed to be as Dewey would have it—ends in view had shaped the means adopted. Unfortunately, however, I had ignored the warning I had received in the form of the groans, that my goals, my "ends in view," were not those of the students; my mind, as Dewey had put it, had not come to "close quarters with the pupil's mind and the subject matter." The lessons I presented were models of perfection (of their type): I lucidly covered centigrade (Celsius) and Fahrenheit thermometers; I had large drawings of both types of thermometers side by side on the chalkboard, with the freezing and boiling points of water carefully aligned; with remarkable clarity, I derived the formula by means of which one could convert a measurement in centigrade into Fahrenheit and vice versa; and—a coup de grace—I passed a thermometer around the class so that everyone could touch the sacred object for themselves.

By the end of the week all seemed to be well—the pupils, by and large, could convert a temperature in one scale into its correspondent in the other, and when asked they could give me the respective boiling and freezing temperatures of water. The following Monday, however, revealed the disaster for what it was. Foolishly, I asked a few questions about temperature before moving on to the next topic on my schedule, and I was amazed at the ignorance that prevailed. Some students (to be honest, many of them) were quite flummoxed that a pot of boiling water could be at both 100 and 212 degrees at the same time! In reflecting on this sad situation, I realized that although I had hoped the pupils would understand the content, the methods I had used were more conducive to the students at best learning by rote—they had put the ideas into "cold storage." Dewey comments on this kind of situation as follows:

> Since aims relate always to results, the first thing to look to when it is a question of aims, is whether the work assigned possesses in-

> trinsic continuity. Or is it a mere serial aggregate of acts, first doing one thing and then another? To talk about an educational aim when approximately each act of a pupil is dictated by a the teacher, when the only order in the sequence of his acts is that which comes from the assignment of lessons and the giving of directions by another, is to talk nonsense.

Dewey remarked—in a passage that at the time I was ignorant of—that if an aim or end in view was genuinely held, then it would also be flexibly held. As he put it in section 2.2:

> The aim as it first emerges is a mere tentative sketch. The act of striving to realize it tests its worth. If it suffices to direct activity successfully, nothing more is required. . . . But usually—at least in complicated situations—acting upon it brings to light conditions which had been overlooked. This calls for revision of the original aim; it has to be added to and subtracted from. An aim must, then, be *flexible*.

So I set about modifying my goals—not only for the unit on temperature (that I decided to reteach), but also for the course as a whole. I resolved to stop worrying about the reactions of external authorities and the course of study they had prescribed—an amount of material that made it inevitable that the coverage would be superficial at best. My aim became leading the pupils to an understanding of the concepts and findings of science that played a role in their daily lives. And since my aim was student understanding, I decided to start with the skills and interests they brought with them to the course—in particular their interest in "making and doing" for themselves. The aim became central to my thinking about means—the aim of achieving understanding of science also became the means I adopted, for the students would achieve understanding as they progressed through the topic. As Dewey's language expresses this point, "An end which grows up within an activity as plan for its direction is always *both ends and means*" (emphasis added).

What happened in the class? I quickly gathered the available personnel together—two part-time laboratory assistants (yes, in those days some schools in Melbourne had lab assistants) and a teacher trainee who was in the school on a "teaching round"—and we worked in groups with the students, doing some elementary glassblowing and producing tubes sealed at one end. These were partially filled with colored water, and the end of each was immersed in melting ice so that the scale mark representing freezing point could be scratched on the glass tube. Boiling point was not so easy to determine, as water does not expand sufficiently—a point that led to an interesting discussion about the virtues of using mercury in a thermometer. And finally the groups of students invented their own scales of temperature measurement, starting with the freezing point of water as zero. One group won a permanent place in my heart by adopting what they called the "Phillips scale," according to which boiling point was 4 degrees. I somewhat undermined the honor that had been accorded me by asking if it would be wise to put one's hand into a bowl of water that was at 3°P—an innocent enough question that prompted a discussion about the purposes that a scale for measuring temperature ought to fulfill. Overall, a worthwhile investment of two weeks seemed to have been made.

To sum up, in Dewey's view having an aim that is held flexibly so that it can change as circumstances require, and using this aim to shape the activities undertaken to attain it, is to act intelligently—and in the long run, it is conducive to survival. Thus the whole account Dewey gives of aims in this chapter is fully consistent with the evolutionary view of mind that he inherited from William James. And Dewey waxes lyrical about it in a memorable passage:

> The net conclusion is that acting with an aim is all one with acting intelligently. To foresee a terminus of an act is to have a basis upon which to observe, to select, and to order objects and our own capacities. To do these things means to have a mind—for mind is precisely intentional purposeful activity controlled by perception of facts and their relationships to one another. To have a mind to do a thing is to foresee a future possibility.

There is one loose end to deal with (if the reader will pardon the pun). Dewey's account of aims or ends or goals seems—up until the final two paragraphs of the body of the chapter—to ignore the fact that often very general or ultimate goals are harbored by humans. His focus throughout has been on aims that are "capable of translation into a method of cooperating with the activities of those undergoing instruction." General or ultimate aims often are not capable of being "translated" in this way, for they may be "detached from all specific context." But here (surprisingly?) Dewey changes his tune and becomes conciliatory. He states that a truly general aim can give educators a broader perspective, opening up new vistas and making them sensitive to a variety of new opportunities. It follows for Dewey that the more general ends we have, the better.

> One statement [of ends] will emphasize what another slurs over. What a plurality of hypotheses does for the scientific investigator, a plurality of stated aims may do for the instructor.

Thus there is no one general aim or end that education serves (a point he reiterates clearly in the opening lines of the next chapter). This, of course, is somewhat jarring to the attentive reader, who will recall that education considered as growth has no end outside itself *apart from* promoting further growth (which certainly seems to be a general or ultimate aim). But it is on this note that the chapter ends—no doubt leaving some readers feeling that what Dewey has given with one hand he has taken away with the other.

9

Natural Development and Social Efficiency as Aims

This chapter has a rhetorical structure that might not be apparent on a first (or even second) reading. This structure is symptomatic of a major intellectual predisposition of Dewey's—which, when it is known by the reader, is the key to understanding a great deal of his writing and thinking. I will reveal this secret key to Dewey more clearly in the next chapter, and just foreshadow it here.

What Dewey is doing in this chapter—hidden by the subheadings he uses—is engaging in a discussion of two pairs of opposing factors, or to use his language, two pairs of dualisms. A dualism is a distinction or an opposition between two entities (for example, between the individual and society), and while it may often be a helpful intellectual device to distinguish between two entities, it also is often a serious mistake to consider the distinction as anything more than a distinction *in thought*; for in reality the two entities may not be separable at all, but may be inextricably interrelated (just as, in the example, an individual is a social individual and is nothing if his or her social attributes and ties are removed; and similarly, society becomes nothing if its constituent individuals are removed from it). Regarding a distinction in thought as being a distinction in the real world is known by philosophers as *reification*.

The two pairs of dualisms Dewey discusses here in chapter 9 are not immediately apparent to the reader because he does not identify them in the section headings, and the three headings he does use give the impression that three things (and not two pairs) are his concern. The three headings are (a) "nature as supplying the aim," (b) "social efficiency as aim," and (c) "culture as aim." But, when examined carefully, his argument will be found to have a different structure: namely, Dualism 1 (*a* versus *b*), nature or the natural versus social efficiency or the social; and Dualism 2 (*b* versus *c*), education for social efficiency or social participation versus education for personal cultural/intellectual development. His argumentative strategy throughout is the same; roughly, he endeavors to make the case that in both dualisms each side or pole has strong and weak points, and the most viable way of resolving the confrontation is to incorporate the strong points of each into a new position—in other words, picturesquely, he proceeds right down the center of each dualism.

Now we turn to an examination of the actual contents of chapter 9. Dewey starts by restating and then amplifying the points he had made about general or ultimate aims in education at the end of the previous chapter. It is futile, he writes, to try "to establish *the* aim of education—some one final aim which subordinates all others to itself." For general aims are perspectives that throw light on different conditions and possibilities, and hence, as he said earlier, there can be any number of them. But then comes a new thought: stating a general aim is an act of emphasis—given the present social circumstances and conditions in which we find ourselves, there is a human tendency to emphasize as goals we want to attain the things we are most lacking. This interesting thesis may well be true about the historical settings in which the examples arose that he discusses at length later in the chapter, but it might be disputed how common a tendency this actually is. Surely we also often emphasize as general goals for the educational process those values and features of society that currently are not lacking but that we judge to be under serious threat and in need of preservation. (Thus, for example, there is much talk in the USA these days that "American values"—whatever precisely these may be—are facing erosion from within and attack from without, and so need to be bolstered by educational and other social institutions.)

After two preliminary paragraphs laying out the thesis described above, Dewey turns to the main purpose of the chapter, which is to discuss three examples of aims that have arisen in the manner described by this thesis. (As indicated earlier, the first and second of these constitute the poles of the first dualism, and the second and third constitute those of the second dualism, as I hope will become clear as we proceed.) He discusses the first of the general aims under the heading "Nature as Supplying the Aim." Dewey points out that educational reformers who "are disgusted with the conventionality and artificiality" of the dominant "scholastic methods" are "prone" to look to nature for the remedy—and he judges Rousseau to be the leading representative of this school. But what are the artificial educational practices that Rousseau and others rejected? Such things as young children in well-to-do families being dressed up—toylike—as little adults, and paraded in front of visitors to deliver recitations or to give mini–musical recitals. And sometimes they were treated as adults where book learning was concerned. A classic example, drawn from a period about two generations after Rousseau's *Emile* was published, perhaps indicates the kind of thing Dewey (and Rousseau) had in mind. In his *Autobiography* (1873), John Stuart Mill (who was born in 1806) describes the education he received when he was a child:

> I have no remembrance of the time when I began to learn Greek. I have been told that it was when I was three years old. My earliest recollection on the subject, is that of committing to memory what my father termed Vocables, being lists of common Greek words, with their signification in English, which he wrote out for me on cards. Of grammar, until some years later, I learnt no more than the inflexions of the nouns and verbs, but, after a course of Vo-

> cables, proceeded at once to translation; and I faintly remember going through Aesop's *Fables* . . . . I learnt no Latin until my eighth year. . . . Arithmetic . . . was the task of the evenings.

In stark contrast to this remarkable but arguably quite "unnatural" education, Rousseau's Emile, unhampered by formal lessons, wandered freely throughout his family's country estate (although accompanied by his tutor). And until late in adolescence he was allowed to read only a single book—one that depicts the kind of life that Rousseau was endorsing, one free of societal influences; it was, of course, *Robinson Crusoe.* (Although it is interesting to note that Rousseau claimed he was dramatizing the principles and did not expect his *Emile* to be considered a practical blueprint for the education of real boys.) Dewey gives a succinct summary of several aspects of Rousseau's educational thought, pointing out that a key element was that the child's (natural) inborn capacities and dispositions should be allowed to develop (naturally) without being subject to social constraints. In a discussion spread out over several pages, Dewey endorses much of Rousseau's position, and he sees Rousseau as making us aware of individual differences and the importance of physical mobility in learning; and of course he recognizes the role played by Rousseau's work in crystalizing a political dogma opposed to "existing social institutions, customs, and ideals" (which will remind some readers that Rousseau has sometimes been called the philosopher of the French Revolution).

Nevertheless there are problems—most notably that Rousseau's "passionate assertion of the intrinsic goodness of all natural tendencies" is hard to sustain, for what makes any impulse good or evil is the social uses to which it is put. Dewey could have gone even further here to point out that "natural tendencies or capacities" often can be identified only by way of, or only can exist because of, social factors or conditions. For example, without the (socially developed and socially recognized) discipline of mathematics, there would be no such thing as "mathematical ability"—just as without the piano there would be no natural piano-playing ability. Furthermore, the fact that some youngsters' natural capacities are neglected or subject to suppression or "premature forcing" (young Mill comes to mind here) does not mean that development of capacities should be left up to "nature," but rather means that we need to struggle to find a more supportive social environment for them. Thus, in terms of the first dualism of nature versus society, while the "nature" pole has much truth to it, it does not embody the "whole truth." And so we arrive at the opposite pole of the dualism, discussed in section 2, "Social Efficiency as Aim."

Those readers who are watching out for it will easily detect at the start of this section a fine example of the way in which Dewey handles dualisms. The strong nature of the thesis that constitutes the first pole, that nature is good and society is evil, "could hardly fail to call out a protest." As a result the opposing pole, the "antithesis," came into existence. This "opposing emphasis"

> took the form of a doctrine that the business of education is to supply precisely what nature fails to secure; namely, habituation of an individual to social control; subordination of natural powers to social rules.

Dewey discusses some of the positive features of this second position, but he also sees drawbacks—for example, education that has the aim of fitting the individual into socially determined roles and modes of behavior favors acceptance of the social status quo, and thus "differences of economic opportunity then dictate what the future callings of individuals are to be."

This second pole of the first dualism also becomes the first pole of the next dualism. For not only is the position that education should have the broad aim of contributing to social efficiency and control opposed to the aim of education being the fostering of natural development of the naturally endowed faculties and inclinations (Dualism 1); it is also opposed to the aim being the fostering of the acquisition by the individual of a personal stock of resources drawn from the culture of the society. (Here one thinks of the totalitarian regimes of the twentieth century, where social control was paramount and where individual freedom to develop was severely curtailed.) Dewey, however, in typical fashion, holds that—if viewed properly—a synthesis of both poles of this second dualism can be embraced, for they are not necessarily in opposition:

> But if democracy has a moral and ideal meaning, it is that a social return be demanded from all *and* that opportunity for development of distinctive capacities be afforded to all. The separation of the two aims in education is fatal to democracy. [Italics added.]

10

Interest and Discipline

Having been regaled with talk of dualisms in the previous chapter, the now sensitized reader will have noted that the title of chapter 10 itself refers to another of this ilk. In its starkest formulation, this is the dualism between, at one pole, doing some task or learning something because you have an interest in it or because it is interesting versus, at the other pole, doing or learning the thing by sheer force of will, by exercising or displaying discipline. This is the dualism that was front and center in the mind of my Latin teacher, all those years ago, who apparently abhorred the "learning Latin because of interest" pole, and instead endorsed (and acted on) the "learning Latin by sheer effort of willpower or discipline" pole. In fact there is a passage a little over halfway through the chapter that in my wildest flights of fancy I suppose could have been written with this very teacher of mine in mind; Dewey points out that for some educators

> application just for the sake of application, for the sake of training, is alone disciplinary. This is more likely to occur if the subject matter presented is uncongenial, for then there is no motive (it is supposed) except the acknowledgement of duty or the value of discipline.

Of course the thought occurs, if only my teacher had read Dewey, he would have realized that he was caught up in a false dichotomy. It is easy to see how a synthesis of the truth in both poles can be accomplished—one can learn Latin, and put all of one's willpower or self-discipline into this, *because* it is interesting.

This is roughly the trajectory followed in chapter 10, although Dewey's discussion is richer than my summary here suggests. His analysis of the concept of "interest" is particularly noteworthy, and I will come back to it later. However, first I must fulfill the promise I made in the previous chapter—namely, that I would reveal in more detail the key to understanding much of Dewey's thought, a key that involves dualisms.

The place to start is by noting that Dewey was part of what the historian of ideas Arthur O. Lovejoy called "the revolt against dualism," and as such he identified and attacked dualisms seemingly whenever possible. Upon consulting the index to D&E, for example, one finds that in this work alone thirty-five of them are critiqued; and many of Dewey's other major works bear titles referring to them—*The Child and the Curriculum*, *The School and Society*, *Experience and Education*, *Experience and Nature*, *Knowing and the Known*, among others. These dualisms embody distinctions that have been accepted widely and therefore have been responsible for misleading generations of philosophers, educators, and laymen.

The next thing to note is that in attacking or critiquing these misleading dualisms, Dewey made use of one or the other or both of two arguments. First, reflecting what has been called a *holistic* position—as we will see below, a position based on Hegel's principle of internal relations—Dewey held that nature is an organic unity or whole, and thus it is only by poetic license, as it were, that we can talk about its "parts." In other words, throughout the natural realm there is *continuity*; what might be thought of as the parts of an organism mutually affect or determine each other, so that in reality they are "organically interrelated"—or in Hegelian terms, "internally related"—and are not separable parts at all. (Dewey had used a variant of this argument to powerful effect in his famous and very influential essay on the reflex arc concept in 1896.) However, to aid in thinking—as an intellectual tool—it is sometimes helpful to distinguish between "parts," but this is a distinction in thought and should not be reified. Furthermore, because the organism is in dynamic interrelationship with the outside environment, the same principle holds here. Overall, as he put it in the fifth paragraph of chapter 24 of D&E, Dewey is highly critical of the "ruptures of continuity" that lead to the establishment of dualisms; and he continues this attack in chapter 25. Furthermore, as we will see later on, he has a helpful example of the danger of reification, centering on eating and digesting, in chapter 13.

The second approach Dewey takes to dualisms is to point out that because in all cases the first pole of a dualism encapsulates only part of the truth, an opposing pole comes into existence that emphasizes the other part of the truth. Thus, it seems to Dewey, the conflict embodied in the dualism can be resolved by finding a position (a "synthesis") that contains the true elements of both poles. And to do this often involves backing off and looking at the problem that generated the dualism in a new way (not always, it must be admitted, an easy thing to do). An important example of this strategy can be found in the influential pamphlet Dewey wrote around the turn of the century—*The Child and the Curriculum* (1902). Dewey describes how two educational sects had formed, one in support of the view that schooling should focus on (at least as a starting point) the interests and experiences of the child, while the rival sect held that schooling should focus on transmitting the fund of knowledge that society had built up over long periods of inquiry (Dewey called this "the curriculum"). Both poles of the dualism have something in their favor, and both face criticisms. How can a mediating synthesis be found?

> What, then, is the problem? It is just to get rid of the prejudicial notion that there is some gap in kind (as distinct from degree) between the child's experience and the various forms of subject-matter that make up the course of study. . . . And we realize that the child and the curriculum are simply two limits which define a single process. . . . Hence, the facts and truths that enter into the child's pres-

> ent experience, and those contained in the subject-matter of studies, are the initial and final terms of one reality.

In short, there is no tension between the interests of the child and the bodies of knowledge that make up the curriculum, because the interests of children, pursued and developed over time, eventually have resulted in the present bodies of knowledge.

The important thing to note here is that both (1) Dewey's holism, and how it led him to be extremely wary of reifying the distinctions we sometimes draw, and (2) his typical way of disarming dualisms, by rejecting both poles and then finding a way to construct a synthesis, are part of the "permanent deposit" that he acknowledged was made to his thinking by the German idealist philosopher G. W. F. Hegel. Hegel argued that all things were organically interrelated and that the only genuine knowledge was knowledge of reality as whole (the "Absolute"); and he also became notorious for using a dialectical method (later adopted, in a modified form, by Karl Marx and then called "dialectical materialism"), whereby a thesis generated its opposite, the antithesis; eventually these were replaced by a synthesis that preserved the truth content of both; this synthesis became the next thesis, and as such it generated its opposite . . . and so the process continued.

It is interesting to note in this context that Herman Harrell Horne's companion to D&E also stresses the Hegelian nature of Dewey's attacks on dualisms and his support of continuity—he writes of D&E that "in succeeding chapters a series of syntheses, in real Hegelian fashion . . . will be effected" (p. 345). Horne was himself an "absolutist" in philosophy, and his companion—published in 1932 but presumably written largely in the year before—bears a dedication marking the centennial of Hegel's death in 1831. It is no surprise, then, that in his judgment, without recourse to an absolutist "system of thought," Dewey is not able to successfully overcome every dualism.

Thus the parallels between Hegel's and Dewey's philosophy are striking—and, as indicated above, were acknowledged by Dewey himself. But there is a twist. Hegel defended his positions by abstract and abstruse argumentation within the framework of philosophical idealism, which at first Dewey accepted. Finally, however, around the turn of the twentieth century, he rejected Hegel's style of arguing. Under the influence of William James, the theory of evolution, and modern biology and social science, Dewey came to see that he could defend holism and attack dualisms more directly and naturalistically in a way that avoided making reference to a metaphysical and transcendental Absolute. As we read on, we will see this shift fairly clearly in chapter 25 in his account of the three factors that have established the principle of continuity. And the autobiographical essay written when he was in his seventies, "From Absolutism to Experimentalism," is also very clear; he put the matter this way:

> I should never think of ignoring, much less denying what an astute critic occasionally refers to as a novel discovery—that acquaintance with Hegel has left a permanent deposit in my thinking. The form, the schematism, of his system now seems to me artificial to the last degree. But in the content of his ideas there is often an extraordinary depth; in many of his analyses, taken out of their mechanical and dialectical setting, an extraordinary acuteness.

This, then, is the key that provides access to Dewey's writings on many topics: He presents the position he endorses as being, in effect, a synthesis that navigates a path between two opposing positions that have been (and that still are) held with respect to the matter at hand. And typically, too, he will discuss the pros and cons of each of these opposing poles, and expose the "evil consequences" to which each of them has led, before he saves the day by putting forward his synthesis. This format served Dewey well for many decades.

To wind down the discussion of chapter 10, we need to return our focus to Dewey's treatment of the concept of "interest." He makes clear that when we pursue a goal or undertake a task out of interest, this does not necessarily mean that "interest" has the sense of "personal emotional inclination." Dewey also points out that the term has a deeper sense in which it means "having an interest, having a stake, in the outcome." But he is crystal clear in rejecting the strategy of providing this stake in the form of an extraneous reward; that is, he rejects the strategy adopted by many teachers of providing students an interest (a stake) in a topic by bestowing an extraneous reward (such as a gold star or "extra credit"). This, he points out in an engaging turn of phrase, is to provide some "pleasant bait . . . hitched to the alien material," and it is to hold a "soup kitchen" theory of education. However, when material connects to the student's current powers and activities and carries these forward, it is not alien and it *is* of interest; the connection "with the promotion of an activity having a purpose is the first and last word of a genuine theory of interest in education," Dewey writes at the end of section 2. Finally, it also should be noted that in section 2 of this chapter Dewey's position once again is founded on the evolutionary view according to which the ability to think—to select goals that are of interest (i.e., in which we have a stake) and then to formulate plans of action to achieve these—evolved because of its great survival value. This view, for example, is just below the surface in the following passage:

> Mind appears in experience as ability to respond to present stimuli on the basis of anticipation of future possible consequences, and with a view to controlling the kind of consequences that are to take place. The things, the subject matter known, consist of whatever is recognized as having a bearing upon the anticipated course of events.

I will pass over, without comment, Dewey's unfortunate use of the term "effeminate" in the third-to-last paragraph of the chapter—it was evidently the product of a shared early twentieth-century insensitivity.

11

Experience and Thinking

This important and philosophically rich chapter starts—once again—with a heading that identifies a dualism! For Dewey's point here is that, in contrast to the common view that thinking occurs after (or prior to) having an experience, thinking is part and parcel of experience; without the involvement of thought or intelligence, experience is simply something that happens to someone, and is not really experience at all. (In other words, as we will see in more detail below, he is rejecting the view of experience held by Locke and many other empiricist philosophers.) He writes in the opening paragraph:

> Mere activity does not constitute experience. It is dispersive, centrifugal, dissipating. Experience as trying involves change, but change is meaningless transition unless it is consciously connected with the return wave of consequences which flow from it. . . . The mere flux is loaded with significance. We learn something.

Given this account, learning from experience involves making a "backward and forward" connection between what we do to our environment and what we "enjoy or suffer" as a result. (Dewey's handling of the reflex arc comes to mind here.) Activity, intelligent interaction with the surroundings, is key; however, learners in school have not been conceptualized as being active inquirers.

Why not? Because traditional thinking has been shaped by what elsewhere Dewey calls "the spectator theory of knowledge"—this is the theory that lay behind the design of that dreadful schoolroom in which I did some of my practice teaching all those decades ago, the schoolroom that was "made 'for listening'" (for to be a listener tightly constrained in a desk is to be a kind of spectator). Dewey's prose here is quite remarkable and is worth quoting at length:

> In schools, those under instruction are too customarily looked upon as theoretical spectators, minds which appropriate knowledge by direct energy of intellect. The very word pupil has almost come to mean one who is engaged not in having fruitful experiences but in absorbing knowledge directly. Something which is called mind or consciousness is severed from the physical organs of activity. . . . The latter [is thought] to be an irrelevant and intruding physical factor.

Dewey asserts that "evil results have flowed" from this "dualism of mind and body." I have no hesitation in pointing out how closely Dewey's exposition here has adhered to the rhetorical pattern discussed in my commentary on the previous chapter.

The body-mind dualism and the spectator theory of knowledge are closely related, and Dewey is right that they have had an important impact on the field of education. (Personally, I also agree with him that this impact has been detrimental.) Since at least the time of Plato, the knower has usually been conceptualized as a physically passive intellect (earlier I referred to Rodin's famous statue, *The Thinker*, which is iconographic of this view of knowledge acquisition). In the allegory of the cave in his masterwork *The Republic*, Plato depicted a group of prisoners chained in a cave so that they could only face the back wall on which shadows of the real world outside were flickering. Much like naïve moviegoers gazing intently at the images on the silver screen, they took these to be actual reality. When their shackles were released so that they could turn around, they saw reality itself—but they still acquired knowledge about it as spectators. Plato did not say they had to act or experiment in the world, venture forth and make changes in it, in order to learn. The prisoners, once released, certainly could venture forth, but they remained spectators. John Locke, another pivotal figure in the history of philosophy, a founder of the modern empiricist tradition, regarded the mind as a "blank tablet" or a cabinet that gets filled with ideas coming from "outside"—a process that, contra Dewey, Locke called "experience." It hardly needs saying that a tablet, or slate, or a cabinet is the epitome of passivity! In Locke's account, mind is active in processing and analyzing ideas only *after* they have been acquired—and this can be done while one is physically quiescent, sitting and contemplating in an armchair (or on a rock, in the case of *The Thinker*).

Dewey holds the completely opposite view, and here again he seems to be indebted to William James. Almost forty years earlier, in 1878, in a review of a book by the British essayist Herbert Spencer in which mind had been depicted as playing a passive role, James—reflecting his view that the ability to think evolved to fulfill the biologically vital role of guiding our activities within the world—wrote in criticism that "the knower is an actor. . . . In other words, there belongs to mind, from its birth upward, a spontaneity, a vote. It is in the game, and not a mere looker on." Clearly Dewey built on this in D&E, and thirteen years later, in *The Quest for Certainty* (1929), this antispectator theory of mind was explained and defended in a discussion that fills several chapters. Near the end of this latter book, Dewey offered the following summary:

> Mind is no longer a spectator beholding the world from without and finding its highest satisfaction in the joy of self-sufficing contemplation. The mind is within the world as a part of the latter's own ongoing process. It is marked off as mind by the fact that wherever it is found, changes take place in a *directed* way. . . . From knowing as an outside beholding to knowing as an active participant in the drama of an on-moving world is the historical transition we have been following [in this book].

In short, we gain knowledge by acting in—making directed changes in—the world and then suffering or enjoying the consequences. To treat the knower or learner as being in principle a physically passive spectator is to make, in effect, both an epistemological and a biological mistake (not to mention an educational one as well).

It is important to insert another cautionary note here: it is easy to get misled by language and to regard mind as a thing, as an object—Dewey himself sometimes uses the word this way, as in the passage quoted above. But in fact he was well aware of the difficulty of using ordinary language, with its built-in supposition that mind and body are separate entities, to express his view that the dualism is false and that we are organic wholes—we are organisms with the ability to think. In other words, for Dewey, rather than the word "mind" naming a thing, it refers to a *capacity*, having the sense of "thoughtfulness" or perhaps "mindfulness."

The point also needs to be made that William James was not the only source inspiring Dewey's stance against the spectator theory. The same lesson came from modern science and its experimental method (as Dewey acknowledged in his preface). Dewey wrote in an important chapter, "The Naturalization of Intelligence," in *The Quest for Certainty*, "Nature is capable of being understood. But the possibility is realized not by a mind thinking about it from without but by operations conducted from within, operations which give it new relations summed up in production of a new individual object."

The "evil results" in the educational domain that Dewey identifies as flowing from the body-mind dualism are right on target. First is the idea that bodily movement is an intruding "distraction" and must be suppressed. Earlier I recounted my own use, as a young teacher, of the "talk-and-chalk" method; my role was to talk and make a chalkboard summary, and the role of the students was to listen and perhaps answer a few desultory questions that chiefly had the function of ensuring that no one had fallen asleep. Furthermore, my training had sensitized me to the dangers of even small amounts of fidgeting, and I cut these off with lightning-like responses—there were to be no such distractions in my classroom! The attentive reader will recall what a dismal failure this approach had been.

Second, historically the dualism led to the senses being "regarded as a kind of mysterious conduit through which information is conducted from the external world into the mind." This is true of Locke's model of the mind as a once empty cabinet furnished with ideas entering via sensory experience; and by the nineteenth century this had morphed into a primitive technique for training the senses—namely, "object lessons." (Again I recall occasionally being subjected to these during my own elementary education.) First devised by Pestalozzi, these lessons were available by the late nineteenth century in numerous books, which spoon-fed the instructor by listing in order the precise questions that had to be asked and the demonstrations that were to be conducted. The idea was simple: the teacher came to class bearing a carefully selected object that was displayed and even—like the thermometer in my ill-fated lesson—passed around so that students could briefly inspect it. The objects used might include such things as a lump of chalk, a piece of glass, a lump of coal, and so forth. A text from 1886, F. Gladman's *School Work*, fills in the details:

> Get children to look at the object, and form ideas about its size, shape, colour and parts. Test them by questions to see how far their idea is accurate and complete, and to exercise them in using words. Direct their observation to points they may have missed. Bring other senses to bear on the object; let the children notice its hardness, softness, elasticity, roughness, smoothness, weight, texture, the sound it emits if struck, its odour.

Gladman justified this procedure in terms of the Lockean model of knowledge acquisition; I do not recall whether my own teacher did the same, but he certainly told us that a series of these exercises would help us think and observe like a scientist. Dewey, of course, held that it was quixotic to attempt to train a faculty like observation in isolation, separated from the relevant subject matter. And in exercises such as those constituting "object lessons," "the senses and muscles are used not as organic participants in having an instructive experience, but as external inlets and outlets of mind." (Before moving on, it is worth noting that Locke's theory of the mind as a blank tablet, and the use of object lessons to train the "conduit" of the senses, will come to the fore again in chapter 20.)

The third evil flowing from acceptance of the body-mind dualism concerns the relations between entities that exist in nature. If asked to provide a list of the kinds of things that are to be found in the natural or "external world," many of us instinctively would give a list of objects—rocks, planets, stars, nebulae, bacteria, types of vegetation, and so forth. But it probably would not occur to many of us to include facts, such as "the Earth is smaller than Jupiter," and law-like regularities. Yet all these things that may have slipped our minds exist, are important, and are things that involve *relations*. Wittgenstein put it memorably in the second sentence of his *Tractatus* (which was written about the same time as D&E), "The world is the totality of facts, not of things." In other words, the world is made up not simply of things but things in relation—and things in relation to one another constitute facts. And, as one might expect, a philosophical puzzle arises here: How, especially according to the empiricist account, is it possible to gain knowledge of these relations?

Let's spell out this problem in a little more detail: According to the Lockean empiricist model, the realm outside of mind ("the external world") is known only by way of the simple ideas that enter the mind via sensory experience, and by way of whatever we then can glean from this input. On this basis we build up (or construct, as modern "constructivists" would put it) a hypothetical picture of reality as composed of objects having primary and secondary qualities. But relationships (such as above, below, before, after, larger, smaller, and so on, as well as a variety of causal connections) are not objects themselves and so cannot give rise to simple ideas in the mind—they cannot "furnish the mind" by way of sensory experience. How, then, do these important things come to be known by us? It must be said that until the twentieth century, philosophy did not do a good job in providing an answer to this conundrum. Locke himself was unclear about his answer to it, but there are places in his work where he holds (the unsatisfactory view?) that relations are produced or constructed *in the mind*—they are relations that the mind sets up between ideas of things. Dewey's account of this unsatisfactory theory, given in the third-to-last paragraph of section 1 of chapter 11, is right on target:

> It is alleged that the mind perceives things apart from relations; that it forms ideas of them in isolation from their connections—with what goes before and comes after. Then judgment or thought is called upon to combine the separated elements of "knowledge" so that their resemblance or causal connection shall be brought out.

Dewey's own answer to the problem is straightforward: the problem "arises in supposing that relationships can become perceptible without *experience*—without that conjoint trying and undergoing of which we have spoken." A mind that is active within the world, and is not merely a spectator but manipulates objects and relationships in a directed manner in an attempt to attain goals, has no problem in principle dealing with relationships. "It is only in experience," he writes, "that any theory has vital and verifiable significance."

We now have arrived at section 2, "Reflection in Experience." Only little by way of commentary is necessary, for Dewey's discussion is clear and flows directly on from the points he makes in the preceding section. He amplifies the theme that thought or reflection does not merely play a role within experience; it is what *makes* experience—it differentiates it from a mere happening. Using the old standby "thus," he writes that "thinking is thus equivalent to an explicit rendering of the intelligent element in our experience. It makes it possible to act with an end in view. It is the condition of our having aims." And, reflecting the Jamesian, or evolutionary, view of the function of intellect, Dewey argues that thinking occurs when we are in situations that are not clear, and where their point lies in how they are going to turn out. Elsewhere he calls these "problematic situations," and he stresses it is the situations that are problematic—the problems are not merely in the minds of the persons involved. He made this quite clear in his book *How We Think*, the first edition of which appeared in 1910; in the opening lines of the summary to chapter 1 of the 1933 edition, he writes that "the origin of thinking is some perplexity, confusion, or doubt. Thinking is not a case of spontaneous combustion. . . . There is something that occasions and evokes it." He also puts this point nicely about halfway through this second section of the chapter we are focusing on in D&E:

> To say that thinking occurs with reference to situations which are still going on, and incomplete, is to say that thinking occurs when things are uncertain or doubtful or problematic. Only what is finished, completed, is wholly assured. Where there is reflection there is suspense. The object of thinking is to help *reach* a conclusion.

And in the next paragraph he adds that "it also follows that all thinking involves a risk. . . . The conclusions of thinking, till confirmed by the event, are, accordingly, more or less tentative or hypothetical."

After dealing with an example, Dewey's discussion in this section ends with a major contribution. He provides a five-step account of the anatomy of a reflective experience, starting with its origin in perplexity generated by one being in an "incomplete situation" that needs to be resolved, and ending with testing one's hypothesis by acting on it. Two important points need to be brought to the reader's attention here. First, this account of a reflective experience easily morphs into a pedagogical guide—it becomes the backbone of the so-called inquiry method of teaching favored by many progressive educators. Second, as a description of a method for resolving problematic situations, the five steps also constitute an account of the scientific method of inquiry. There is proof here of the truth in the old adage that "great minds think like," for one of the great philosophers of science of the twentieth century, Karl Popper, independently gave an uncannily similar account of this method in chapter 4 of his book *Objective Knowledge* (1972). Popper summarized his theory in the form of a flow diagram:

P (1) → TT → EE →P (2)

Thus, problem solving begins with an initial problem (P [1]), followed by formulation of a tentative theory or hypothesis about the solution (TT), which is followed by severe critical examination and testing—or error elimination (EE)—which then may result in a reformulated problem (P [2]), and so inquiry continues. Popper says curtly that "this schematic analysis is very widely applicable"—a judgment that Dewey might well have endorsed. However, perhaps the most significant point of agreement between these two giants of twentieth-century philosophy is that inquiry starts with a problem.

12

Thinking in Education

In this chapter Dewey discusses the educational ramifications of the philosophical points he made in chapter 11. His theme is that fostering the ability to think is of paramount importance, but it cannot be accomplished in isolation from contexts of action where there are genuine problems to be solved. Similarly, the knowledge that also is required for problem solving cannot be acquired in isolation from such contexts. In the opening paragraph, Dewey pens some memorable prose on this point:

> Information severed from thoughtful action is dead, a mind-crushing load. Since it simulates knowledge and thereby develops the poison of conceit, it is a most powerful obstacle to further growth in the grace of intelligence.

Later, at the end of point 2, he uses another memorable expression to refer to this "mind-crushing" load, an expression which I must admit is my favorite in the whole of D&E: it is a "*static, cold-storage ideal of knowledge*," wherein information is "heaped up" and filed away in storage until a display of it is "called for" (italics added). Such information has not "functioned in experience through use in application to the student's own purposes," and so it clutters up the mind like "miscellaneous junk."

Dewey's discussion of these and similar matters in this chapter is clear and often engaging, but he fails to illustrate his points with examples. I step forward to remedy this omission.

The first exhibit is drawn again from my own experience as a high school student. In years eleven and twelve, through no fault of my own, I was placed in the math/science "track," but my budding academic career was nearly shipwrecked on the rocks of a yearlong twelfth-grade course in chemistry. The teacher had a good reputation, but he was near the end of his career and it was clear even to us students that he was burned out. The course was a demanding one with a syllabus handed down from the external curriculum authority; we were expected to be familiar with the details of what seemed like an infinite number of chemical reactions and tests, along with their relevant chemical equations. In the parallel physics course, we had at least one lengthy laboratory session each week, but in the chemistry class, the whole year passed without us ever touching even a test tube. For our teacher had opted to demonstrate the relevant chemical tests and reactions from the bench at the front of the lab while we pupils took notes—he seemed to have judged this to be much more efficient time- and effort-wise than allowing thirty pubescent teenagers to run amok in the laboratory. Although, on the whole, the thirty of us did very well in the end-of-year statewide competitive exams in pure mathematics, calculus, and physics, only three passed chemistry. I was not one of them. In Dewey's terms, the problem was obvious—the large amount of material in the course had not "functioned in experience through application" to my own purposes; instead it was presented for what it was—"a mind-crushing load." I had no interest in the material, and I noticed that—try as I might, and despite having a good memory (no thanks to Latin)—I simply was unable to commit most of the chemical reactions to memory, for my mind seemed to become a complete blank. And as I reflected later, what also amazed me was the fact that as many as three of my classmates had managed to file the stuff away in storage and were able to recall it later for use in the external examinations. (Fortunately, the story has a happy ending; at the university the following year,

I took a yearlong chemistry course at a higher level, one with six hours of lab work per week in which the theory was learned in a context of application, and I did well enough to expunge the blot on my record.)

My second exhibit is drawn from early in my academic career when, as a young faculty member in a school of education, I visited trainee teachers on their practice-teaching rounds in local schools. On the occasion I have in mind, however, I was visiting the school to watch a lesson by a "master teacher" who was regarded as innovative and "up and coming," and who was about to supervise a couple of trainees in our program. As his students entered the classroom, they were confronted by a large laboratory-style bench at the front of the room, bare except for a lonely, large glass flask that contained a colorless fluid. After the class members quieted down, the teacher's instructions were simple: "Break up into your usual lab groups, take a sample of the fluid from the flask, and find out what is in it." For the next forty minutes there was about the usual level of background noise that accompanies group work, but as I wandered around the room and eavesdropped on the students, I decided the conversations were more about movies and football scores than they were about the makeup of the mysterious liquid. The students were minimally engaged because the problem that had been set had no connection with their experience—it was a schoolroom problem, not a *real* one. As Dewey put it about halfway through section 1,

> Is it the pupil's own problem, or is it the teacher's or textbook's problem, made a problem for the pupil only because he cannot get the required mark or be promoted or win the teacher's approval unless he deals with it?

How different would the exercise have been, I mused, if the teacher had collected water from the nearby creek that no longer harbored tadpoles, frogs, and fish; or if (in a flight of fancy) the teacher claimed the liquid had been taken from the stomach of a person who had died under mysterious circumstances? (For how many teenagers don't like a good mystery?) My disillusion with this classroom episode, and its lack of context for the (pseudo)problem that had been set, reached a new low when later I asked the teacher to explain the reasoning behind his lesson plan; his answer—that the aim was to allow students to practice acting like scientists—would have made Dewey and Popper cringe (for according to their analyses, inquiry always starts with a genuine problem that needs to be solved).

For my third and final exhibit, I return the reader to the chalk-and-talk lesson I delivered about thermometers, and which I discussed in my comments on chapter 8. It was a good lesson *of its type*, for—as my questioning at the end of the week indicated—the students had successfully acquired a "heap" of cold-storage knowledge from which they could retrieve relevant items when given the right cues ("what is boiling point on the Fahrenheit scale?"). Unfortunately—as I discovered the following Monday—they did not understand the material, and were unable to act on it, because it had been presented to them in a context that did not involve their direct interest or experience or need to act. In Dewey's terms, I had taught in a way that did not encourage genuine thinking on the part of my students. I thought I had transmitted *ideas* to them, but Dewey (and William James) would disagree, for according to the pragmatists, an idea is a "plan of action" and its function is to guide our actions in a productive way. Without the student thinking and wrestling with a problem, the "idea" being transmitted is a lifeless fact. All of this was revealed to me on that fateful Monday when I gave my students slightly different cues, when I asked questions that were phrased slightly differently from the language on the labels of the materials in cold storage—and the students were not able to locate the desired items.

Another example occurs to me here: Consider two different ways of learning how to put together a piece of furniture. The first method is by attending a lecture on how to do it, when you do not own or intend to purchase the item in question; the second is to have hands-on access to the item—which you have just purchased—while you are consulting the printed directions.

The first method almost certainly will lead to complete withdrawal, and virtually no learning will occur. The second method will surely be far more successful—despite occasional bursts of frustration when you find you do not have enough nuts and bolts to complete the assembly (or worse still, that you have too many left over)—and the skill acquired might, with luck, be transferable for use on other items.

I have one more confession. Later in my teaching career, I recognized that another point Dewey makes in this current chapter applies to my original lesson about thermometers; he put it this way in a passage about five paragraphs before the end of the chapter,

> There can be no doubt that a peculiar artificiality attaches to much of what is learned in schools. . . . It assuredly does not possess for them [the students] the kind of reality which the subject matter of their vital experiences possesses. . . . They become habituated to treating it as having reality for the purposes of recitations, lessons, and examinations.

Chapter 12 ends with the usual summary, but it is unusual in that Dewey devotes very little space to summarizing the points he has made; instead, without explicitly referencing it, he harks back to the five-step analysis of a reflective experience that he gave near the end of the previous chapter. His reasoning is this: "thinking is the method of an educative experience"—by which he means that sans thinking there is no educational gain, and the experience is not even a genuine experience but is just a "happening." He continues: "The essentials of method are therefore identical with the essentials of reflection." Here we see, in essence, that a philosophical analysis has become a pedagogical blueprint—a matter that Dewey explicitly addresses in famous words in chapter 24: "Philosophy may even be defined *as the general theory of education*." But some treats must be left for later.

13

The Nature of Method

Although a faithful companion on a long and complex journey is expected to provide an interesting perspective (though no doubt it will sometimes be mistaken) on the highlights that are encountered on the way, occasionally he or she may be left speechless when a confusing vista opens up. Such is (almost) the case with me and the present chapter. Although over the years I must have read it upwards of forty times, I still get stalled by what seems to be an insurmountable problem. I wish the reader better luck than I have had in resolving it.

The problem, of course, is what Dewey means by "method"—method of, or method for, what? Undoubtedly in the course of the chapter several clear and important points are made, but this fundamental puzzle remains throughout. In different places Dewey seems to be referring to different things. And if they are not different, at least he owes us a clear explanation of what he means.

Consider the long opening paragraph. In summary the argument is that subject matter and method are inseparably connected; trying to separate them creates an unsustainable dualism according to which "method then has for its province a consideration of the ways in which this antecedent [independent] subject matter may be best presented to and impressed upon the mind," which in turn suggests that a "complete theory of methods of learning" can be "deduced" without any "knowledge of the subjects to which the methods are to be applied." Dewey judges this position to be completely mistaken; his message is that methods of learning (whatever this expression might mean—perhaps he really means methods of teaching?) are subject matter *dependent.*

In the next two paragraphs the following account is presented. Dewey states that the

> fact that the material of a science is organized is evidence that it has already been subjected to intelligence; it has been methodized, so to say. . . . Method means that arrangement of subject matter which makes it most effective in use.

Here Dewey is giving (at least) two different accounts of "method," accounts which happen to be different from the one he gave originally. First, the way in which a subject—quantum mechanics, for example, or string theory—is ordered internally is a matter determined by the logic or theoretical structure of the discipline; this can be different from, second, the way in which it is ordered for ease of use where the interest may not lie in the nature of the theory's structure but in its practical applications; and the ordering for ease of learning and perhaps for effective teaching (Dewey's original account) are different yet again. It may be helpful here to contemplate the difference between an advanced research monograph on quantum theory and an entry-level textbook treatment of the subject.

More awaits us. A little further on in the chapter, Dewey uses the case of "eating and food" as an example of a dualism that in some contexts is helpful but which is quite misleading if taken too seriously. He uses this (somewhat mysteriously?) to introduce another distinction: namely, the one between

> *what* we experience (the experienc*ed*) and the experienc*ing*—the *how*. When we give names to this distinction we have subject matter and method as our terms. There is the thing seen, heard, loved, hated, imagined, and there is the act of seeing, hearing, loving, hating, imagining, etc.

Method as "how we experience" is yet another sense of the term, and one that some readers will need further help to understand (but unfortunately this is not forthcoming).

Near the end of section 1, in subsections 3 and 4, Dewey adds to the confusion. He indicates he is discussing "methods of teaching a child" (to read); but then, half a page later, "method tends to be reduced to a cut and dried routine" whereby students (yes, students and not their teachers) are led to believe there is one fixed method to be followed; then a few lines later Dewey criticizes the practice of "handing out" to teachers "recipes and models to be followed in teaching." Instead, the method of teaching must be seen as "the method of an art, of action intelligently directed by ends." A little more than a page later Dewey states:

> Education also has its general methods. And if the application of this remark is more obvious in the case of the teacher than of the pupil, it is equally real in the case of the latter. Part of his learning, a very important part, consists in *becoming* master of the methods which the experience of others has shown to be most efficient in like cases of getting knowledge.

Still referring to the student, Dewey opines that "imposing an alleged uniform general method upon everybody breeds mediocrity in all but the very exceptional."

As a last resort, an appeal to the chapter's summary for further clarification yields only this: "Method is a statement of the way the subject matter of an experience develops most effectively and fruitfully." At this point, speechless and disoriented, I must change the topic.

14

The Nature of Subject Matter

The summary at the end of this chapter does its job well—it gives a comprehensible and concise account of the matters that are dealt with. It is clear here, as indeed it is in the body of the chapter, that Dewey is adopting a social perspective toward the subject matter of instruction. In essence there is a link to the theme of the very first chapter of D&E, where he stressed that education is the process by which society renews itself, for (as he puts it in the closing paragraph of that chapter) "what nutrition and reproduction are to physiological life, education is to social life." At the end of chapter 14 he makes a related point:

> The subject matter of education consists primarily of the meanings which supply content to existing social life. The continuity of social life means that many of these meanings are contributed to present activity by past collective experience.

The chapter opens with Dewey giving a "genetic" or historical account of the evolution of subject matter—a kind of creation story. It is quite general in nature—no historical evidence from any actual society is referred to—but nevertheless the account is quite plausible. In the beginning, in primitive societies, most of the meanings (knowledge) and skills that were required for survival of the individual and the group were acquired by youngsters by way of their participation in the activities of adults (such things as hunting and gathering of edible and medicinal plants). A few things crucial to group cohesion and survival, such as religious beliefs and stories about ancestors, cannot be learned in this way, and these were passed on to the new generation during their preparation for, and participation in, initiation rites and the like. As societies became more complex, a great amount of knowledge and skills, based on "ideas deposited from past experience" (of the group) accumulated, and this material became "more definitely formulated for purposes of instruction." The invention of writing boosted this process, and so formal subject matter of instruction evolved. Eventually the origin of this material in actions that contributed to group survival and cohesion was lost sight of; as Dewey nicely phrased it:

> Finally, the bonds which connect the subject matter of school study with the habits and ideals of the social group are disguised and covered up. The ties are so loosened that it often appears as if there were none; as if subject matter existed simply as knowledge on its own independent behoof.

At this stage we are only three paragraphs into the chapter, but the discerning reader already will have an inkling of the kinds of educational "consequences" for which Dewey is preparing the ground.

Before turning to these, however, a few other matters need to be raised. First, whereas Dewey sees the subject matter of instruction (elsewhere called the "curriculum") as being a very important tool of social reproduction, many curriculum theorists (a few earlier, and many later in the twentieth century) have gone further and have regarded it as a tool of social control—a very powerful one because it appears to be so benign and its true nature lies hidden, disguised by a justificatory "legitimation narrative." Michael Apple, a prolific writer on these matters, expressed it this way in *Official Knowledge* (1993, pp. 55–56):

> The selection and organization of knowledge in schools is an ideological process, one that serves the interests of particular classes and social groups. However, as I just noted, this does not mean that the entire corpus of school knowledge is "a mirror reflection of ruling class ideas, imposed in an unmediated and coercive manner." Instead, "the processes of cultural incorporation are dynamic, reflecting both continuities and contradictions of that dominant culture and the continual remaking and relegitimation of that culture's plausibility system."

Another influential tradition—emanating chiefly from economists of education—sees the school curriculum as a tool to be used to achieve national economic prosperity. Yet others (such as myself) see little difference between these two traditions. And there remains one other prominent group of philosophers of education that sees the curriculum as containing a set of cultural resources that students can draw on as they develop personal autonomy.

Finally, before returning to Dewey and the educational consequences he sees flowing from his analysis of subject matter, attention should be drawn to the underlying logic of his argument, about which some readers might have a sense of unease. This form of argument—a genetic argument—is far from rare in Dewey's writings. Stripped to its bare bones, it runs like this: In the past, an item (I) evolved in a social group or species to fulfill the vital function (F); if this function still needs to be fulfilled and if no better way has developed, then the use of (I) must be fostered or preserved with this function as its main priority. Thus, in the present case, subject matter knowledge, item (I), developed in a social context where survival of the group depended on its members acting as if they *belonged* to a social group, which is the function (F), and (I) helped achieve this. Therefore (the argument runs) the item (I) must be passed on with this purpose uppermost. There is, however, a response to this: one key to historical and even evolutionary progress is that the item (I), after it has evolved of course, can acquire new functions, (G), (H), . . . , that equip the group or its individual members to face the conditions that prevail at the present time (think of the new functions acquired by the human hand, with its opposable thumb, after it evolved from the more primitive appendage possessed by our primate forebears which had a limited range of possible functions). Finally, sometimes the old function (F) might have faded in importance or new ways of achieving it might have been developed (think of the ways government propaganda agencies, newspapers, TV, and other mass media have taken on the task of promoting social identity in modern societies).

The point here should not be lost—it is not that Dewey was wrong, but that the *form* of his argument is not as compelling as he seemed to assume. It is worth noting, in passing, that Herbert Spencer, the great British essayist of the second half of the nineteenth century, used a similar although not identical evolutionary/genetic argument in his attempt to establish the priority of importance among subjects on the curriculum (an argument that helped place the sciences ahead of the classics in the popular mind).

Returning to the body of Dewey's chapter, we see that from the fourth paragraph on he considers some of the educational consequences of the position he has just sketched. He starts by adopting the perspective of the instructor, and he makes several points here—the second of which is central to much of his thinking about educational practice, and the discussion of which runs over several paragraphs. His point is that the organized subjects as they currently exist are not suitable for direct transmission to students, but rather should be regarded as resources or guides for the instructor. Dewey makes his case with some fervor:

> From the standpoint of the educator, in other words, the various studies represent working resources, available capital. Their remoteness from the experience of the young is not, however, seeming; it is real. The subject matter of the learner is not, therefore, it cannot be, identical with the formulated, the crystallized, and systematized subject matter of the adult; the material as found in books and in works of art, etc. The latter represents the *possibilities* of the former.

Although the teacher should have "subject matter at his fingers' ends,"

> the teacher should be occupied not with subject matter in itself but in its interaction with the pupil's present needs and capacities.

This position has been influential down to the present day. For example, it is reflected fairly accurately in the well-known work of Lee Shulman and his colleagues, according to which the educator needs to have "pedagogical content knowledge." It is worth quoting Shulman's original formulation of this quite Deweyan notion at some length; within this category, he wrote,

> I include, for the most regularly taught topics in one's subject area, the most useful forms of representation of those ideas, the most powerful analogies, illustrations, examples, explanations, and demonstrations—in a word, the ways of representing and formulating the subject to make it comprehensible to others. Since there are no single most powerful forms of representation, the teacher must have at hand a veritable armamentarium. . . . Pedagogical content knowledge also includes an understanding of what makes the learning of specific topics easy or difficult: the conceptions and preconceptions that students of different ages and backgrounds bring with them. ("Those Who Understand: Knowledge Growth in Teaching," *Educational Researcher* [February 1986]: p. 9)

In the middle third of the chapter, Dewey switches to adopt the perspective of the learner. The knowledge people first acquire, he asserts, is "knowing how to do"; the natural course of development always sets out from "situations which involve learning by doing." And in a nice turn of phrase, Dewey states,

> Only in education, never in the life of farmer, sailor, merchant, physician, or laboratory experimenter, does knowledge mean primarily a store of information aloof from doing.

By now the reader will be alert to the fact that this, also, is a type of genetic argument: the order or way in which some complex process originated or occurred in the past is the order or way in which it should take place today. I leave it up to the reader to sort out the pros and cons here; but I daresay that the education of the young John Stuart Mill is worth reconsidering in this context. Meanwhile, our journey continues.

The second point Dewey makes in this section is that personal doing—the basis of knowing—involves intercommunication with others; during this process some of the vast store of "social knowledge" that has accumulated over time is passed on to the young learner. This process continues in school. It is easy "to swamp a pupil" with this transmitted information, unless two criteria are met:

> Does it grow naturally out of some question with which the student is concerned? Does it fit into his more direct acquaintance so as to increase its efficacy and deepen its meaning? If it meets these two requirements it is educative.

Nevertheless, the "imposing stupendous bulk of this material" has shaped (or rather, misshaped) our attitude toward subject matter. This information is divided into various branches of study, and then subdivided further into "lessons presenting in serial [order] cut-off portions of the total store." And so "acquisition of a modicum of information in each branch of learning" remains the principle on which the school curriculum is based.

It is a saddening account, but one which has a great deal of face validity. And Dewey has put his finger on a problem that many educational theorists and philosophers struggled with in the following decades. The situation is even more dire than Dewey depicted—in some fields (currently biology probably is the most notorious) knowledge is doubling every five years or less. (Philosophy, I am happy to say, is progressing somewhat more sedately.) How, then, can this "mind-crushing load" be passed on to students? About half a century after the publication of D&E, a number of philosophers of education and curriculum theorists tackled this problem using the notion of "structure." As I put it elsewhere,

> They focused on the nature of knowledge itself; and they decided that bodies of knowledge have certain important structural features, and that furthermore there are only a small number of different *types* of knowledge. . . . The structure of a branch of knowledge is conferred upon it by its concepts and their interrelationships." (*Philosophy, Science, and Social Inquiry* [1987], p. 123)

The important British analytical philosopher of education Paul Hirst, using structure as his guide, sorted all the fields of knowledge into seven different types or forms (mathematics, physical sciences, human sciences, history, religion, literature and the fine arts, and philosophy). Students should become well-enough acquainted with one subject from each of these seven forms of knowledge that they can make a meaningful decision about whether to keep studying that particular form. (This was a heaven-sent analysis for British curriculum authorities, as typically there were seven periods in the high school daily schedule!) Another approach, also based on the notion of structure, held that teaching in any subject should focus on transmitting structural understanding—for when students understood the key concepts and the types of relationships between them, the tests against experience that were used to distinguish truth from fiction, and suchlike, they would be equipped to understand any future developments that would occur within the subject in question. As the (then) Harvard psychologist Jerome Bruner wrote, a student who understood the structure of the discipline he was working within, was

> well on his way toward being able to handle a good deal of seemingly new, but in fact, highly related information. . . . Grasping the structure of a subject is understanding it in a way that permits many other things to be related to it meaningfully. (*The Process of Education* [1963], p. 7)

In the 1960s several massive curriculum development projects, in the USA and UK, were mounted based on these ideas of Hirst and Bruner. Some of the issues relevant here will be taken up later in chapter 21.

In the third section of the chapter, Dewey turns his attention to one particular branch of subject matter—"science or rationalized knowledge." This comes somewhat as a surprise, and the discussion fits a tad uncomfortably with what preceded it (the discussion of science later, in chapter 17, or in chapter 21 where the clash between science and the humanities is tackled, might have been better placements). Nevertheless, here it is in chapter 14.

In essence, Dewey's discussion in this present section centers on a distinction made more explicitly, and certainly more clearly, by later analytic philosophers—namely, between knowledge (or knowing) and belief (or believing). This distinction is often expressed in the form of the so-called justified true belief (JTB) analysis of knowledge. Simply put, according to this account, if you were to claim that you knew (had knowledge of) item X—for example, that "the Earth revolves around the Sun," or "the Earth is roughly spherical in shape"—then three conditions must be met: first, you must believe X; second, X must be true; and third, you must possess some evidence or justification for claiming X is true. The argument for this analysis is straightforward—if you do not believe X, you can hardly claim to know it (for it is apparent that this would be contradictory); if X is not true, you cannot know it to be the case (for you cannot know something that is not the case—you cannot know the Earth is a large cube, because it is not so—although, it is crucial to note, you certainly might *believe* this false item); and even if X is true or is the case, and you believe X, you cannot claim to know X unless you have some justification. An example should make this third condition clearer. Suppose that you believe that there is some form of life on the planet Jupiter (condition 1), and suppose also that this happens to be true (condition 2); this remains a *belief* that happens to be a lucky guess unless you have some valid grounds for this belief (indeed, without some evidence or justification, you would not even be sure that your guess was "lucky"). Without some type of reasonable justification, you cannot claim to *know* that there is life on Jupiter, no matter how strongly you believe this to be the case.

It might seem that this discussion has taken us far from Dewey, but not so! His point in this section is that science is the form of knowledge on which we can act confidently, because its claims have been tested adequately; and he warns against prematurely abandoning the testing process. What comes to mind here is the importance Dewey assigned to the experimental method of knowing in his preface to D&E. And in one of his subsequent books, *Logic: The Theory of Inquiry* (1938), he writes at length of the need to have a proper warrant for each of our assertions, and the method of experimental testing used in science—a method that involves acting on an assertion or belief and noting the outcome—is the best method we have for producing such warrants or authorizations for our assertions. The following very significant passage occurs about halfway through section 3 of chapter 14 of D&E:

> Without initiation into the scientific spirit one is not in possession of the best tools which humanity has so far devised for effectively directed reflection. One in that case . . . fails to understand the full meaning of knowledge. For he does not become acquainted with the traits that mark off opinion and assent from authorized [warranted] conviction.

This important chapter ends with a brief section discussing "subject matter as social." Dewey's point is straightforward: while all subject matter has been developed in a social context and with social resources, and is transmitted by social means, it is not all of equal social importance. A selection has to be made. Again there is a fervent quality to his prose:

> The scheme of a curriculum must take account of the adaptation of studies to the needs of the existing community life; it must select with the intention of improving the life we live in common so that the future will be better than the past.

15

Play and Work in the Curriculum

According to an old adage, play is the child's work. If we were to add to this that work is the adult's play, we would have a pithy statement that comes close to capturing Dewey's position in this chapter. In effect he is arguing that setting up a sharp distinction—a dualism—between play and work is a mistake; but he does make the case that it is important to distinguish between work and drudgery, as well as play and fooling around. He gives a forthright statement rejecting the dualism at the start of section 3, using the term "industry" as a synonym for "work":

> In their intrinsic meaning, play and industry are by no means so antithetical to one another as is often assumed, any sharp contrast being due to undesirable social conditions. Both involve ends consciously entertained and the selection and adaptations of materials and processes designed to effect the desired ends. The difference between them is largely one of time-span.

The words "undesirable social conditions" refer to a point Dewey touches on in a couple of places in the chapter—namely, that what he calls the evils of the industrial system sometimes are such that workers labor under conditions where they lack control over their ends (and the means to these ends). "Under unfree economic conditions," he says near the end of the chapter, "this state of affairs is bound to exist." He continues:

> Work or industry [then] offers little to engage the emotions or the imagination; it is a more or less mechanical series of strains.

In short, under such conditions work has become drudgery—and it has lost the features that make it similar to play.

I will not offer a summary or précis of Dewey's argument in this chapter, but I will do what (once again?) he fails to do—namely, discuss a few examples. Consider first the out-of-school context. Here, for Dewey, "play" does not mean such things as idly throwing pebbles into a pond or kicking a can around a field; these are merely fooling around. By "play" he seems to mean such things as make-believe shopkeeping, making a tree house while pretending to settle in the jungle (Tarzan movies have a lot to answer for), or sliding down a hill on a sheet of cardboard in an attempt to scoot over a stream at the bottom (Evel Knievel has even more to answer for). And "work," in the out-of-school context, is exemplified for Dewey by such things as a carpenter producing a customized piece of furniture or a service mechanic performing maintenance on the engine of a passenger jet. In all these cases (both play and work) the ends in view are not separate from the processes or means that are used but rather infuse them; the participants take pride in the activities involved; the activities and the ends are social in character; the activities involved are intrinsically motivated (remuneration may be involved, but is not the sole or determining factor); and participants acquire skills, knowledge, facility in using tools, and even knowledge of some laws of nature during these activities that, in both cases, "are carried on [in some degree] for their own sake." As the activities involved in children's play become more complicated, play gradually transforms into work.

Of this analysis of the similarities between play and work, what is the significance for schooling? In Dewey's view,

> it is the business of the schools to set up an environment in which play and work shall be conducted with reference to facilitating desirable mental and moral growth. It is not enough just to introduce plays and games, hand work and manual exercises.

For the problem with these activities is that they too readily become focused on predetermined steps and procedures; their social significance is lost sight of, and intelligence and imagination are not called forth in the students. Instead, Dewey argues, "occupations" should be made use of. His discussion of these here in chapter 15 is not as thorough or compelling as the treatment he offered about fifteen years earlier in *The School and Society*; to whet the reader's appetite, I offer this passage from the start of chapter 6 of this earlier work:

> By occupation is not meant any kind of "busy work" or exercises that may be given to a child in order to keep him out of mischief or idleness when seated at his desk. By occupation I mean a mode of activity on the part of the child which reproduces, or runs parallel to, some form of work carried on in social life. . . . The fundamental point in the psychology of an occupation is that it maintains a balance between the intellectual and the practical phases of experience.

In section 2 of chapter 15 of D&E, Dewey provides a list of occupations that could be used, and offers some advice about how they should operate in school so as to maintain their educational benefits, and to his credit, Dewey develops at some length the example of gardening.

The chapter eventually circles back to work and drudgery—the latter arising when the ends of activity are externally imposed and its social significance is lost sight of. (It has often seemed to me to be a pity that, in later reprints of D&E, Dewey did not use as an example at this point the wonderful, scathing, and hilarious depiction of a factory assembly line in Chaplin's famous film *Modern Times*.)

The chapter closes with a minor rhetorical flourish:

> Work is psychologically simply an activity which consciously includes regard for consequences as a part of itself; it becomes constrained labor when the consequences are outside of the activity as an end to which activity is merely a means. Work which remains permeated with the play attitude is art.

Dewey of course was not the only philosopher in the modern era to be concerned about work as drudgery or as constrained labor—although he might have been alone in using "play" as a foil in his argument. The tendency among other writers and social critics has been to frame the issue as involving worker alienation and lack of autonomy. In addition to Chaplin, the Marxist tradition comes to mind here; why Dewey did not refer to it is a minor mystery.

16

The Significance of Geography and History

In this chapter Dewey discusses two subject matter areas that subsequently have undergone something of a reversal of fortune. Geography has almost ceased to exist as a separate academic field and consequently as a subject in the school curriculum—most university departments have disappeared, for example—although some of its subspecialties have been absorbed by the likes of economics and geology departments and school subjects such as social studies. History now has a less dominant place in the curriculum, and anecdotal evidence indicates that—in the context of the US high school—many students dislike American history and judge it to be boring.

Dewey regards both subjects as important, but the rationale for teaching them has become obscured. "The words 'history' and 'geography,'" he wrote near the beginning of section 2,

> suggest simply the subject matter which has been traditionally sanctioned in the schools. The mass and variety of this matter discourage an attempt to see what it really stands for, and how it can be so taught as to fulfil its mission.

He points out, however, that seeking a deeper significance for history and geography is often seen as "a vain fancy."

Vain or not, Dewey of course steps into the breach. He claims that our mundane "narrow personal action" and activities involving "mere forms of technical skill" gain depth of meaning when set into the wider context of time and space provided by geography and history—providing, of course, that these are properly taught. In Dewey's words,

> With every increase in ability to place our own doings in their time and space connections, our doings gain in significant content. . . . Thus our ordinary daily experiences cease to be things of the moment and gain enduring substance.

But he goes on to issue this warning:

> Of course if geography and history are taught as ready made studies which a person studies simply because he is sent to school, it easily happens that a large number of statements about things remote and alien to everyday experience are learned. . . . Mere amassing of information apart from the direct interests of life makes mind wooden; elasticity disappears.

Later in the chapter, midway through section 2, he lets loose his rhetoric; if its human ties are lost sight of, geography

> presents itself as that hodge-podge of unrelated fragments too often found. It appears as a veritable rag-bag of intellectual odds and ends: the height of a mountain here, the course of a river there . . . the boundary of a country, the capital of a state.

How, in Dewey's view, should geography be taught? Local or home geography, he says, is the natural place to start—but it is not an end in itself, rather "it is an intellectual starting point for moving out into the unknown." Once again I volunteer an example. I have a vague recollection of hearing about (or reading about) a teacher who was about to embark on a series of lessons concerning the location of major US cities, state boundaries, and the like. Instead of presenting the students with a map and having them learn by rote a hodgepodge of facts—"here is where New York is located," "here is Chicago"—she presented them with a map that only displayed physical features such as rivers, mountains, plains, coast line ocean depths, and the like. She then asked the students to role-play being an emperor sending new settlers to this land: "Where would you suggest the major cities be built, and why?" This led to some lively discussions about the need for fresh water, ease of transport and communication, likely places for agriculture and grazing, and so forth; the resulting map was compared with a map of the USA, and the location of cities on both were discussed. The series of classes ended with the teacher and students exploring the reasons for their own town's location. This seems close to what Dewey had in mind—but if not, at least my example is extremely Deweyan in spirit!

Geography studies the physical setting or environment in which our lives take place; and history has for its ambit the social setting. But, as with all dualisms, Dewey rejects setting up a boundary, and he argues that the natural or physical realm "is the medium of social occurrences." He elucidates further:

> When this interdependence of the study of history, representing the human emphasis, with the study of geography, representing the natural, is ignored, history sinks to a listing of dates with an appended inventory of events, labelled "important"; or else it becomes a literary phantasy.

Dewey proceeds in section 3 of the chapter to make some points about the nature and importance (or lack of it) of historical knowledge that some later critics have judged to be crass or at least narrowly utilitarian. But it also can be argued that Dewey was being a consistent pragmatist, holding firmly to the philosophical position that the function of thought (including ideas and knowledge) is to give intelligent direction to the actions we undertake in the future in order to solve the problems we currently face. Thus the worth of an idea lies in its usefulness in the future, not in where it came from.

The section starts rather uncompromisingly with Dewey rejecting, in effect, studying "history for history's sake"—that is, studying it because it is intrinsically interesting in itself, or because it reveals the many forms that human societies can take, or because it displays the diverse motivations that have shaped human behavior:

> The segregation which kills the vitality of history is divorce from present modes and concerns of social life. The past just as past is no longer our affair. If it were wholly gone and done with, there would be only one reasonable attitude toward it. Let the dead bury their dead.

The next sentences, however, are more positive.

> But knowledge of the past is the key to understanding the present. History deals with the past, but this past is the history of the present. . . . The true starting point of history is always some present situation with its problems.

It seems clear that the pragmatic functionalist philosophy of mind lies just below the surface here.

In subsequent paragraphs Dewey comments on various forms of history—biographical, industrial and economic, intellectual, and so forth. He warns against using history as a "reservoir of anecdotes to be drawn on to inculcate special moral lessons on this virtue or that vice." However, history is a "permanent and constructive moral asset" if it contributes to "a more intelligent sympathetic understanding of the social situations of the present."

It would be remiss of me if I did not mention, before concluding, the strong objection taken to Dewey's view of history by the great twentieth-century British philosopher and logician Bertrand Russell. Although I hesitate to say so of a man whose work I generally admire, I find his opinion of Dewey simply bizarre. In his wonderfully readable *History of Western Philosophy*, in the chapter on Dewey, Russell accuses him of "cosmic impiety," by which he means that Dewey holds the "god-like" view that truths about the past can be made false (and vice versa) according to whether they suit one's human purposes in the future.

> The main difference between Dr. Dewey and me is that he judges a belief by its effects, whereas I judge it by its causes where a past occurrence is concerned. . . . Dr. Dewey holds that it has "warranted assertibility"—which he substitutes for "true"—if it has certain kinds of effects. . . . But if truth, or rather "warranted assertibility," depends on the future, then, in so far as it is in our power to alter the future, it is in our power to alter what should be asserted. This enlarges the sense of human power and freedom. Did Caesar cross the Rubicon? I should regard an affirmative answer as unalterably determined by a past event. Dr. Dewey would decide whether to say yes or no by an appraisal of future events.

Once again, in Deweyan spirit, I rely on you—the reader—to reach your own conclusion. May the force be with you!

17

Science in the Course of Study

Dewey had extremely high regard for science—both the results that it had obtained and the method it had developed to guide inquiries so that the final results would be well warranted. This is very clear in his preface and in the opening sentence of the present chapter:

> By science is meant . . . that knowledge which is the outcome of methods of observation, reflection, and testing which are deliberately adopted to secure a settled, assured subject matter.

Given this, it is somewhat surprising to find that his discussion in chapter 17 is rather pallid compared with the more robust prose he uses in works such as *Reconstruction in Philosophy*, *The Quest for Certainty*, or *Logic: The Theory of Inquiry*. For example, there is nothing in the present chapter of D&E to rival the prose in chapter 3 of *Reconstruction*, where Dewey writes (near the end) that the "revolution in our conception of nature and in our methods of knowing it has bred a new temper of imagination and aspiration." And

> education and morals will begin to find themselves on the same road of advance that say chemical industry and medicine have found for themselves when they too learn fully the lesson of whole-hearted

> and unremitting attention to means and conditions—that is, to what mankind so long despised as material and mechanical.

For millennia humans lived in a "tight and pent in universe" where possibilities were fixed, but now—thanks to science—we live in a natural world that is "relatively malleable and plastic" and therefore improvable. Here Dewey had a noble, modernist vision of a "brave new world," untarnished at that time by any sign that science eventually would come to be regarded by many as a dark force that erodes values, beliefs, and practices that ought to be preserved.

Let's now return to chapter 17. The discussion opens with Dewey distinguishing between the "logical" and the "psychological" orientations toward science (although this is an analysis that can be applied to any body of subject matter, as soon should become apparent). Dewey was in fact revisiting in a rather muted way a distinction that, thanks to the brilliant example of an explorer and a map, he had explicated more effectively in his pamphlet *The Child and the Curriculum* (1902). To avoid misunderstanding, the reader should note that Dewey is not using "logical" in the sense of referring to the subfield of philosophy, but rather is using it in a more general sense of referring to "relations between, or organization of, the parts" (as in, for example, "the logic of the layout of goods in the nearby supermarket").

Imagine, then, that there is an explorer who is venturing out into new terrain. Typically an explorer keeps a diary or log of daily experiences—the events that occurred, the sights seen, the hazards encountered, and so on; essentially this is a "psychological" (some might say "phenomenological") record of the experiences of the explorer. Eventually an analysis of these experiences will take place; this is a reorganization that replaces the daily, or (as Dewey also calls it in D&E) chronological, order of events and hazards with a textbook-type organization that represents their locations spatially or geographically. In other words, a map will be produced that lays out a "logical" ordering of the features encountered.

These "two are mutually dependent," Dewey writes in *The Child and the Curriculum*, for without the more or less accidental wanderings of the explorer, there would be no facts that could be used to produce the chart, but without the chart, later travelers would glean no benefit:

> The map orders individual experiences, connecting them with one another irrespective of the local and temporal circumstances and accidents of their original discovery.

Studying the map, Dewey warns, is no substitute for the personal experience of the journey through the terrain—studying a map of Melbourne, or reading a text about it, is no substitute for visiting that fair city. But to visit without a map is to deny oneself the benefit of what has been learned by previous travelers:

> the map, a summary, an arranged and orderly view of previous experiences, serves as a guide to future experience; it gives direction; it facilitates control; it economizes effort, preventing useless wandering.

My high school chemistry teacher, discussed in an earlier chapter, could have profited from reading about the explorer and the map (about the psychological and logical ordering of subject matter). He believed he could demonstrate the logical ordering of the subject to his students, without allowing us to get firsthand (psychological) experience of the terrain—and he was horribly mistaken. On the other hand, the science teacher I observed, who put a flask of clear liquid in front of his students and then let them loose, placed them in a situation where they would have firsthand experience of the terrain (or rather, the experience of being lost in the terrain), but where they were unable to get guidance from a map—and a great deal of "useless wandering" ensued.

All of this is part of what Dewey is conveying in the first section of chapter 17. And there are flashes of first-rate prose as he ventures a little further; for example, when discussing logical form he says:

> There is a strong temptation to assume that presenting subject matter in its perfected [logical] form provides a royal road to learning.

> What more natural than to suppose that the immature can be saved time and energy, and be protected from needless error by commencing where competent inquirers have left off?

Dewey warns that if taught in this manner, "the pupils learn a 'science' instead of learning the scientific way of treating the familiar material of ordinary experience," and given that most of them will not become scientists, the latter—knowledge of the scientific method—is much more relevant. And if the early stages of science education are not based on personal experience with material of "ordinary acquaintance," Dewey claims students likely will suffer "the mental confusion and intellectual distaste attendant upon studying matter whose meaning is only symbolic." Once again my high school chemistry class rears its ugly head.

In the second section of the chapter, on "science and social progress," we find a clear statement of Dewey's meliorism—this being the philosophical position that the world is neither good nor bad, but can be made better by human efforts. (Some less charitable commentators will phrase this differently; they claim it is more accurate to classify Dewey as a modernist with an unbridled belief in progress. So be it.) Dewey also makes the point that science not only provides us with the means to achieve the ends we harbor, but—even more crucially—it allows us to formulate *new* ends or goals. And surely there are innumerable examples from contemporary life that indicate Dewey was right about this.

The final section of the chapter deals with a dualism that has a centuries-long history in the curriculum field, namely, "the humanities versus the sciences." I personally fell afoul of this dualism in the final two years of my high school education—I was nudged, rather firmly, into the "science track" despite the fact that I felt rather drawn toward the humanities. But they were, in my day, two totally independent steams—indeed, at that time I would have had to relocate to a different high school to pursue work in the humanities. And the "Berlin Wall"–type division between the two traditions continued at the university—only a very few brave souls managed to escape across in one direction or the other. Modestly I will not indicate whether I was one of them.

Thus, like Dewey, I regard the dualism as invalid; but frankly, if I were captain of a team debating this issue, I would hate to have Dewey on my side. For on this occasion I find his attack on the dualism rather weak and/or poorly formulated. But once again I leave the matter up to the reader to decide (although another chance to consider the relevant issues will arise in chapter 21).

18

Educational Values

For many years, I had to take a deep breath when I reached this chapter in D&E, for I knew I would have to work through it several times in order to grasp what was going on. At last I have had a breakthrough, which I will attempt to share.

The difficulty in coming to grips with this chapter is not that Dewey's prose is particularly murky; rather, the difficulty seems to emanate from the fact that his "enemy"—the position he is critiquing—remains partially hidden, and furthermore, the issues being discussed are ones unfamiliar to many contemporary readers. This, I should hasten to add, is not to say that the prose is always transparent. Instead of phrasing his points positively and straightforwardly, here he often states them negatively, which sometimes obscures the meaning. And passages like the following (a single sentence!) do not serve well to deliver Dewey's message; they require at least several readings by mere mortals such as the author of your companion:

> We are thus met by the danger of the tendency of technique and other purely representative forms to encroach upon the sphere of direct appreciations; in other words the tendency to assume that pupils have a foundation of direct realization of situations sufficient for the superstructure of representative experience erected by formulated school studies.

However, all is not lost, for the main enemies appear one at a time; and Dewey has the helpful tendency to make the points that matter to him in several different ways. And these points are, indeed, important.

The first section is titled "The Nature of Realization or Appreciation," which at first blush is difficult to associate with the chapter heading, "Educational Values." His point here is that educational values, which often are embedded in the aims that are held, are mere words unless they are "realized" or appreciated; "internalized" would be a more modern formulation perhaps (Dewey says a synonym would be something like "really taking it in"). And to appreciate values in this way requires what Dewey calls "imagination." It is probably not quite hitting the target, but it is close, to say that Dewey's enemy here in section 1 is "paying lip-service to values, and not really appreciating their import." For example, I believe that ever since my undergraduate days I have valued clarity of expression; but at first I held this more or less as a mantra. I did not realize what "clarity" meant (and that it *applied to me!*) until I received back from my supervisor draft chapters of my master's thesis covered with comments in red ink saying things like "This sentence has four possible meanings—am I supposed to guess what you mean?" and "This is vague and is a cop-out!" I am not sure that "imagination" is quite the right term for the cause of this epiphany, but this is the one that Dewey uses.

He also is of the opinion that holding values in this appreciative way is easier in (or perhaps it is only possible in?) domains where we have had direct experience; but many bodies of subject matter in the modern world are known to us chiefly through the medium of language and other symbol systems—and this exacerbates the problem:

> There is always a danger that symbols will not be truly representative; danger that instead of really calling up the absent and remote in a way to make it enter a present experience, the linguistic media of representation will become an end in themselves. . . . The only way to appreciate what is meant by a direct experience of a thing is by having it.

In short, reading about forgiveness or integrity is not the same as experiencing such a virtue firsthand, and certainly reading does not *replace* experiencing.

In section 2 the focus shifts to "the valuation of studies." The framework for the discussion is the traditional distinction between intrinsic and instrumental values—the first being values that are good in themselves, values whose worth is independent of external events or consequences; and the second being values that are not good in themselves but which are instruments that help produce something that is intrinsically good. Thus, health is intrinsically good, while taking (as I do) a massive daily dose of vitamin pills—while not good in itself—is an instrumental value insofar as it helps produce health.

Dewey does some interesting things with the aid of this distinction. First, he points out that it is futile to attempt to evaluate our intrinsic values in order to determine the hierarchy of their importance (that is, to determine if some particular intrinsic value or good is better than another). This is futile—indeed, misguided—simply because all of them *are* intrinsically good. (It would be rather like trying to rank ten objects in order of their monetary value when each is worth one hundred dollars.) However, second, it *is* possible to rank these values *given a specific context or problem situation*. When one is stranded in a conflict zone with a small band of compatriots, to use an example I must admit I have only read about, the intrinsic good of "being charitable to thine enemy" might play second fiddle to the intrinsic good of "sharing with one's friends those resources that are vital for survival." Thus, given the nature of the specific problems being faced in a particular situation, one intrinsic value might stand out head and shoulders as the best as an *instrument*!

Whom is this philosophical armamentarium directed against here in section 2? Who or what is the enemy? It is anyone who tries to "establish a hierarchy of values among studies" (that is, among subjects on the curriculum). For knowing each of these subjects is good in itself, and intrinsic goods cannot be compared in this way.

> It is futile to attempt to arrange them in an order, beginning with one having least worth and going on to that of maximum value. In so far as any study has a unique or irreplaceable function in experience, in so far as it marks a characteristic enrichment of life, its worth is intrinsic or incomparable.

However, in a specific context it may be the case that one of these intrinsic goods is a better instrument than the others for reaching some goal, so that in specific contexts the intrinsic goods or values can be arranged in different hierarchies. Thus, for Robinson Crusoe on his desert island, soon to be attacked by hostile cannibals, while all subjects on the curriculum may be equally valuable, in this context science probably is a better bet as an instrument increasing chances of survival than are poetry and art and algebra. Later, when celebrating his survival, music might rise to the top of Robinson's hierarchy.

Let's give a face to the opponent here in section 2: it is the British essayist Herbert Spencer. In the late nineteenth century, among the educated portions of world society, Spencer was an incredibly well-known "public intellectual"; and the collection of four of his essays about education—titled *Education: Intellectual, Moral and Physical* (1861)—soon was translated into some fifteen languages and was influential worldwide. The best-known essay in this work was, significantly, "What Knowledge Is of Most Worth?," and in this Spencer attempted to do what Dewey claimed was impossible. Spencer sorted the tasks of life into the order of their evolutionary importance, which coincided with the order in which they had surfaced in the history of the human race—"those activities which directly minister to self-preservation" being at the top, and "those miscellaneous activities which fill up the leisure part of life" being at the other end. In an individual's education, attention should be "greatest where the value is greatest, less where the value is less, least where the value is least." According to Spencer's analysis using this schema, the subject which was of most worth and which should receive the main emphasis in education was, of course, science. (Dewey, it is relevant to note, used science as a specific example about halfway through section 2, very likely with Spencer in mind; furthermore, Spencer's emphasis on science and downgrading of the classics rules him out as being the author of the long quotation three paragraphs into section 3.) At first sight Spencer's position might seem to be quite close to that held by Dewey, but there are important if subtle differences—which again I leave to the reader to sort out.

Section 3—"The Segregation and Organization of Values"—keeps the focus on Spencer, without mentioning his name. The reference to the famous essayist is clear enough in the opening sentences: "It is of course possible to classify in a general way the various valuable phases of life. . . . There is some [educational] advantage in such a classification." However, there is danger here too:

> But it is a great mistake to regard these values as ultimate ends to which the concrete satisfactions of experience are subordinate.

Dewey goes on to discuss one problem that certainly can be identified with Spencer's approach to curriculum—namely, the

> tendency to segregate educational values due to the isolation from one another of the various pursuits of life. The idea is prevalent that different studies represent different kinds of values, and that the curriculum should, therefore, be constituted by gathering together various studies till a sufficient variety of independent values have been cared for.

And later he repeats the point: according to this mistaken approach, "an ideal education would then supply the means of meeting these separate and pigeon-holed interests."

One problem with this general (Spencerian) approach is that the curriculum suffers from "congestion"; it gets packed with separate, isolated studies. But the main problem is that the values and interests embedded in experience cannot justifiably be separated and pigeonholed in discrete subjects—for as quoted above, the activities of life cannot be segregated neatly from each other. In the second-to-last paragraph of the section, Dewey writes that each subject in the curriculum is mistakenly treated as contributing "to the others only externally and accidentally." The point seems to be that all subjects have a number of values embedded within them—intellectual, aesthetic, social, economic, and so forth—that can be displayed depending on context and how these subjects are taught. Furthermore, the subjects interact with, and contribute to, each other: science has an aesthetic side, as does mathematics; and science interacts with theology and history, and of course with mathematics; history also has links with mathematics, art, and literature, as well as with science . . . An example Dewey uses here (although he makes it a tad difficult to follow by stating it negatively) is as follows: even business can be studied in a way that fosters a broadening of the imagination, and that opens up possibilities for it to contribute to social service, and so on—it is a mistake to regard it as only relevant to the amassing of money.

And so the chapter ends. But the ever-alert reader is in for a surprise. In the bottom half of the final paragraph of the summary, Dewey sneaks in what he seems to believe is a fact about social groups; he asserted this in the opening lines of the second-to-last paragraph of section 3, but it remained a conjecture, as he did not undertake the difficult task of providing a justification or warrant for it. I italicize the passage for those whose concentration is lapsing:

> The tendency to assign separate values to each study and to regard the curriculum in its entirety as a kind of composite made by the aggregation of segregated values *is a result of the isolation of social groups and classes.*

Dewey, however, makes (partial?) amends for this sin of omission in the following chapter.

19

Labor and Leisure

The point of this chapter is clear, as is the prose—and therefore lengthy commentary is not called for. As the chapter title indicates, the topic here is another harmful dualism—one that, in Dewey's judgment, is "probably the most deep-seated antithesis" in the history of education. But "education in preparation for useful labor" versus "education for a life of leisure" does not reflect merely a conflict of values—in the spirit of the final lines of the previous chapter, Dewey asserts that this antithesis reflects a "division within social life."

Dewey uses as an example—running over several pages—the social structure of ancient Greece and the assumptions that underlay it, and how this structure was reflected in Greek philosophy, particularly in the writings of Plato and Aristotle. The separation of liberal education from "industrial" education goes back to these ancient times, and the distinction was "formulated expressly on the basis of a division of classes into those who had to labor for a living and those who were relieved from this necessity." This distinction between labor and leisure, made on the basis of social divisions in an ancient society, has been influential for more than two thousand years. Over several pages Dewey probes it further, showing that the life of reason became associated with the leisure class, and how a further division arose between those who used reason in the affairs of life and those who worked "within" reason itself (the thinkers and philosophers). Turning to the present day (1915), Dewey remarks at the start of section 2:

> That the actual social situation has greatly changed since his [Aristotle's] day there is no need to say. But in spite of these changes . . . there remains enough of a cleavage of society into a learned and an unlearned class, a leisure and a laboring class, to make his point of view a most enlightening one from which to criticize the separation between culture and utility in present education.

The situation has slightly improved, he remarks a couple of pages later, but "the idea still prevails that a truly cultural or liberal education cannot have anything in common, directly at least, with industrial affairs."

My own elementary and high school education, more than three decades after the publication of D&E, certainly is illuminated by Dewey's analysis. At the end of sixth grade, I said farewell to many of my school friends, who were channeled off to a technical high school that trained them for a life as electricians, plumbers, carpenters, and shopkeepers. Along with three others, I was directed into the academic high school some miles away. It all seemed so natural! In this academic environment, we were divided even more, into A, B, C, and D tracks. At first, to my mortification, I was not placed in the A track, but this horrendous mistake was corrected after the end of the second year of high school. At home, at last, in the top academic track, I discovered that the foreign language that we had to study (and it was *only* the top track that was allowed to learn it), was . . . (Here I pause to remind the reader that this exciting story is set in Australia, which is located just south of Indonesia, and only a little farther removed from China—but halfway around the globe from France, Germany, and Great Britain.) Yes, the language was—Latin! Our curriculum did not include economics, bookkeeping, comparative religion, world literature, or the history of our corner of the globe. However, we did study physics, chemistry, several branches of mathematics, and the British romantic poets. I still know more about the kings and queens of Britain than I do about the history of the Asian countries. Looking back, I get the feeling that Dewey was absolutely right when he said, about the modern school curriculum, that

> our actual system is an inconsistent mixture. Certain studies and methods are retained on the supposition that they have the sanction of peculiar liberality, the chief content of the term liberal being uselessness for practical ends.

Not only is the curriculum as a whole an "inconsistent mixture," but the muddle also is reflected *within* individual subjects. Dewey says about halfway through section 2 that

> it would be hard to find a subject in the curriculum within which there are not found evil results of a compromise between the two opposed ideals. Natural science is recommended on the ground of its practical utility, but is taught as a special accomplishment in removal from application.

It is clear what Dewey would like to see happen; adopting his usual strategy for resolving dualisms, he argues that we must come to recognize that "only superstition" makes us believe that a subject cannot be both liberal and useful at the same time. In this spirit, he ends on a high rhetorical note:

> The problem of education in a democratic society is to do away with the dualism and to construct a course of studies which makes thought a guide of free practice for all and which makes leisure a reward of accepting responsibility for service, rather than a state of exemption from it.

The question that remains is whether the situation has changed significantly in the century since Dewey wrote D&E, or in the six decades or so since I traversed my way through elementary and high school education. An important new player on the educational scene is, of course, computer and communication technology; but there are some commentators who worry that in this context knowledge becomes a commodity, something to be "googled" in digestible chunks and "on demand" to fulfill some utilitarian purpose, just as a pizza can be called forth by using the appropriate "app." In other words, is the "knowledge for its own sake" side of the dualism fading away? I leave such matters to be pondered by readers who are more up to date than yours truly.

20

Intellectual and Practical Studies

The title of this chapter creates the expectation that it will contain a discussion that follows on from the previous chapter, for "intellectual and practical" seems closely related to "labor and leisure" (or rather, "leisure and labor"). But, as one reads on, this expectation is soon dashed—the chapter might more accurately have been called "A Brief History of the Concept of Experience: From Plato to Locke and Beyond," or even "Reason, Knowledge, and Experience," either of which would have made clear that this chapter is closer in spirit and content to chapter 11 than chapter 19.

Given the vast historical sweep, Dewey does a remarkable job; in clear prose, marred only by a lack of references and illustrative quotations, his case develops in three stages. He starts with the world of ancient Greece, where it was held that only the use of reason could lead to true knowledge, and that experience could only lead to acquaintance with the ever-changing, and inferior, empirical world; then he jumps to the late seventeenth-century world of John Locke and the eighteenth-century world of his successors in France, where a reversal of views occurred and experience rather than reason was the ultimate source of knowledge of the real, external world. While this constituted an advance, the concept of experience that was harbored was (to use the technical philosophical label) a form of sensationalism—it was regarded as the passive absorption of sensations or impressions that entered the receptive mind of a spectator by way of the conduit of the various sensory pathways. Finally, experience was realized to be an active or experimental affair, wherein the knower made changes to, or acted on, the environment and "suffered" the consequences—and thereby gained knowledge. Much of Dewey's story is by now familiar to the reader, for as indicated above, its elements have been met earlier in D&E.

In section 1, then, Dewey discusses the "opposition of experience and true knowledge" that existed in Greek thought and which was articulated in the philosophy of Plato. He gives an account of the "grounds for the identification of experience with the unsatisfactory condition of things, the state of affairs represented by rule of mere custom"—an account that draws on the social structure of Greek society, where artisans were lower in the hierarchy than were the men of leisure who could devote much of their time to study and philosophical discourse. A few lines from Plato's *Republic* capture the difference between the (abstract) realm of genuine knowledge and the (worldly) realm of empirically or experientially derived opinion: "When the mind's eye rests on objects illuminated by truth and reality, it understands and comprehends them, and functions intelligently; but when it turns to the twilight world of change and decay, it can only form opinions, its vision is confused and its beliefs shifting" (6.508). Dewey expounds this Platonic view in the first eight or so paragraphs of chapter 20—and there are numerous passages here that almost match Plato in their rhetorical quality.

Although the position just outlined has not been the dominant one in the modern world, it is by no means dead and buried. Recall that in the previous chapter I recounted how many of my elementary school classmates were "siphoned off" at the end of grade 6 and sent to a lower-status technical high school where they became immersed in the "twilight world of change and decay"; but this is not the end of the anecdote. Many years later, when I had finished my university training and five years of service as a high school science teacher, and was a full-time doctoral student, I had occasion to call an electrician to fix some minor household problem. (Only foolhardy amateurs meddle with electricity in Australia, where the voltage is a deadly 240v!) He turned out to be one of my long-lost school friends. During our conversation while he was doing the repairs, he impressed me with his "rule-of-thumb" knowledge about electrical circuitry, his knowledge of "Ohm's Law" and other formulae. However, when pressed, he admitted that he did not understand the theories (and research) that linked these—nor, he proclaimed, did he care! The rule-of-thumb knowledge worked well enough for his purposes. On the other hand, armed with a science degree with a minor in physics, I believed that I understood the theory, but I was a complete ignoramus when it came to making a household repair. I consoled myself with the thought that I was the one who had genuine knowledge, while he, burdened with mere opinion, had to be satisfied with carrying away a goodly chunk of money. To mark the occasion—*which* had a great impact on me and provoked much reflection—I insisted on naming the newly acquired family cat Plato.

In the second section of the chapter, Dewey turns to the "almost complete reversal of the classic doctrine of the relations of experience and reason" that took place in the seventeenth and eighteenth centuries. In the space of a few pages, he tells a readable but inevitably short and simplified story leading to the rise of the experimental method, the denouement that he reaches in the following section. More recent scholarship shows how complex the matters he touches on really were, and the interested reader is referred to Stephen Toulmin's book-length discussion of the same period in *Cosmopolis: The Hidden Agenda of Modernity* (1990), or to relevant chapters of John Passmore's *The Perfectibility of Man* (1972).

According to Dewey's account, to the "modern reformers" of the seventeenth and eighteenth centuries,

> reason, universal principles, *a priori* notions, meant either blank forms which had to be filled in by experience, by sense observations, in order to get significance and validity; or else were mere indurated

> prejudices, dogmas imposed by authority, which masqueraded and found protection under august names. The great need was to break away from captivity to conceptions which, as Bacon put it, "anticipated nature" and imposed merely human opinions upon her.

Continuing on in the important opening paragraph of section 2, Dewey says that, for these reformers, the important thing was to "resort to experience to find out what nature was like." However, these reformers did not win the battle between reason and experience quite as easily as perhaps Dewey's general account suggests; the tribulations of Galileo at the hands of the Inquisition come to mind—particularly revealing about the strength of the opposition is the anecdote about the refusal of one cardinal to look at the heavens through Galileo's telescope for himself (because, in light of reason and Scripture, he already knew the truth). Nevertheless, the case of those stressing the primacy of experience came to predominate.

The empiricist philosophy of John Locke and his successors in Britain and on the Continent, however, conceptualized experience as being sensory experience—that is, the passive absorption by the "blank tablet" of the mind of sensations (sensory impressions) coming "in" via the five senses. And Dewey points to what he (rightfully) regards as a serious defect here:

> According to the theory there was no need of thinking in connection with sense-observation; in fact, in strict theory such thinking would be impossible till afterwards, for thinking consisted simply in combining and separating sensory units which had been received without any participation of judgment.

In short, for Locke and others, having experience is not an active affair—it does not involve bodily or mental activity, and the recipient of experience is in effect a spectator. Processing of the sensations can take place after their absorption into the mind, for the mind has inborn faculties or powers. (The modern analogy that you may recall I am fond of using is that of the smartphone; it comes out of the package without specific content in its memory—this has to be keyed in by the user—but it has prewired into it a number of powers such as the ability to perform multiplication and division, play video clips, and search for items on the web. It is indeed an electronic Lockean device!)

Two interesting aspects of the post-Lockean history of sensationalistic empiricism are briefly touched on by Dewey in the third and fourth paragraphs of section 2, and are worth a little amplification. First, the mystery of the origin of the seemingly "inborn" powers was given a thoroughly sensationalistic explanation by Étienne Bonnot de Condillac. In 1754 he postulated the following striking thought experiment: Imagine a marble statue of a man that was endowed in turn with each of the five sensory pathways. As the statue was given each of these senses, it not only would acquire a variety of ideas from the outside world, but it would also acquire the various intellectual powers—for intellectual powers or faculties are also the product of sensory experience. (I must confess that, try as I might, I cannot quite grasp the nature of the miracle that must occur in the process Condillac describes.) Second, Helvétius (1715–1771) believed that, as the contents of the mind were the products of sensory experience, and as in principle the sensory experience of individuals could be controlled or at least manipulated, the possibility arose that mankind could be perfected through education. He wrote:

> If I can demonstrate that man is, in fact, nothing more than the product of his education, I shall doubtless reveal an important truth to mankind. They will learn that they have in their own hands the instrument of their greatness and their felicity, and to be happy and powerful nothing more is requisite than to perfect the science of education. (*A Treatise on Man* [1810/1969], vol. 1, p. 3)

Realizing how radical this view was, to escape persecution, Helvétius arranged for his work to be published only after "its author be no more."

Dewey's verdict on the account of experience given by supporters of sensationalism was clear; as he put it at the start of section 3, it represented "neither the idea of experience justified by modern psychology nor the idea of knowledge suggested by modern scientific procedure." With regard to psychology, Dewey of course was writing before the work of the developmental psychologist Jean Piaget, but their views were strikingly similar: both men realized that rather than being passive spectators who merely absorbed sensory input, infants were active learners—touching and grasping and manipulating objects in the environment. Dewey's prose here rises to the occasion:

> It would seem as if five minutes' unprejudiced observation of the way an infant gains knowledge would have sufficed to overthrow the notion that he is passively engaged in receiving impressions. . . . For it would be seen that the infant reacts to stimuli by activities of handling, reaching, etc., in order to see what results follow upon motor response to a sensory stimulation.

The "logical outcome" of the emergence of modern psychology and experimental science was the development of a new view of experience, in which it is seen to be "a deliberate control of what is done with reference to making what happens to us and what we do to things as fertile as possible." And although Dewey does not say it, this is consistent with the pragmatists' evolutionary theory of the origin of the human ability to think—namely, that this capacity arose because it has great survival value in the hostile environment in which we live.

Eventually Dewey relates all of this back to the purported topic of the chapter; the link is that intellectual gain comes about from engagement in activities in the world—in short, it is artificial to separate intellectual and practical work. He writes in the final paragraph before the summary:

> The most direct blow at the traditional separation of doing and knowing and at the traditional prestige of purely "intellectual" studies, however, has been given by the progress of experimental science. If this progress has demonstrated anything, it is that there is no such thing as genuine knowledge and fruitful understanding except as the offspring of *doing*.

21

Physical and Social Studies: Naturalism and Humanism

On this journey through D&E I have, in general, been admiring of Dewey's many insights in the preceding chapters—insights which often have been expressed in inspirational prose. But honesty requires that I draw the line with this chapter. There are several groups of problems with it. One set stems from Dewey's characteristic manner of setting out his argument, which simply does not work in this case. And the second set relates to the fact that the content of the chapter just has not aged well—too much water has flowed under the bridge since 1915 when Dewey was crafting his discussion. Yet, despite the defects, the chapter has one feature of enduring importance: it points to a serious and as yet unresolved problem—one that had been tackled briefly in an earlier chapter—namely, the bifurcation of the sciences and the humanities (or the dualism between the naturalistic studies and the humanities) as areas of study in schools and universities.

In outline this chapter seems straightforward enough, and it is wise to get oriented by starting one's reading with the summary. The philosophical "dualism between man and nature," Dewey says, is "reflected in the division of studies between the naturalistic and the humanistic." Dewey traces the fortunes of this distinction from the ancient world down to his own time, noting that modern science was born in the Renaissance and that it was the "the daughter of humanism," yet it quickly became alienated from its parent. In the modern world, this separation has been reflected in educational practice, where the tendency has been to

> treat the sciences as a separate body of studies consisting of technical information regarding the physical world, and to reserve the older literary studies as distinctively humanistic.

Dewey is extremely light on details, but apparently he believes the dualism can be overcome by teaching science in such a way that its social (and therefore humanistic) importance becomes evident. As he expresses it about halfway through section 3,

> The obvious pedagogical starting point of scientific instruction is not to teach things labeled science, but to utilize the familiar occupations and appliances to direct observation and experiment, until pupils have arrived at a knowledge of some fundamental principles by understanding them in their familiar practical workings.

He suggests that courses that would fit the bill here could start by focusing on such things as the gasoline engine, the telephone, or the electric motor. In sum, then, education (he says a little earlier in the section)

> should aim not at keeping science as a study of nature apart from literature as a record of human interests, but at cross-fertilizing both the natural sciences and the various human disciplines such as history, literature, economics and politics.

On the other hand, Dewey also acknowledges that interested students should have a chance to "advance to specialized ability in science," but he gives no detailed advice as to how the different desiderata he has mentioned can be either reconciled or achieved.

I pointed out in earlier chapters that, in setting up and then critiquing a harmful dualism, Dewey often adopts what philosophers call a genetic approach—one that traces the origins or genesis or history of the matter under examination. In the present case the story covers about 2,300 years of Western intellectual history, and Dewey treats it at an extraordinarily high level of abstraction. He does not anchor his discussion by making reference to examples from the vast number that are available; he does not name, let alone quote, any ancient Greek or Roman authors (except Plato), thus giving the impression that there was unity of opinion among them, when this was not the case; nor—apart from a brief mention of Francis Bacon—does he discuss any Renaissance figures (surely a mind-blowing defect when the topic is the relationship between the humanities and modern science), or any from the nineteenth century; and he does not cite any secondary sources (of the hundreds available) except Hatch and a mere phrase from Windelband! All of this makes the chapter seem aloof, divorced from reality, which is extremely jarring in a writer who holds that philosophy should be rooted in the affairs of the real world and not in some supermundane realm of vague generalities.

Dewey cannot be held accountable for the second set of defects in this chapter, for—not being blessed with the gift of second sight—he could not foresee the developments that would occur in the decades after the publication of D&E in 1916. (Although perhaps he might have had premonitions after reading Mathew Arnold, Thomas Henry Huxley, John Henry Newman, Herbert Spencer, and others, and given the late nineteenth-century debates in Germany about the scientific and humanistic credentials of economics and social science, disputes with which he was probably familiar.)

Perhaps the main event that occurred during the twentieth century, one that helped change the focus of the debate, was the extremely rapid development of the sciences, and the accompanying staggering accumulation of scientific knowledge. On a very conservative estimate, the amount of scientific information has doubled at least every ten years, although I recall seeing, a few years ago, a report saying that the amount of knowledge in biology was doubling every five years. Using the more conservative figure, this means that in 2016 curriculum developers in the sciences have had to deal with about one thousand times more material than was known when D&E was published! How to pass on to the rising generation the enormous and rapidly expanding stock of knowledge became a pressing issue in the second half of the twentieth century, as did the related problem of how to prepare students to deal with the future developments that were approaching at the speed of an express train. One approach that emerged a decade or so after Dewey's death in 1952, outlined in my discussion of chapter 14, was to focus science education on imparting an understanding of the so-called structure of science.

Dewey's own statement about the right way to proceed, in the opening lines of the fourth paragraph of section 2, does not seem to be true given the situation in the sciences today, and might not have been true in the sciences around 1915:

> The utilization of ordinary experience to secure an advance into scientific material and method, while keeping the latter connected with familiar human interests, is easier today than it ever was before.

Certainly it makes sense in many courses (and not only in the sciences) to start off with some problem or example that will be familiar to the students because it is part of their own everyday experience. But is it indeed easier now to do this than it was in yesteryear? Rather, it seems to be the case with many topics throughout the sciences of today that the treatment will be quite superficial unless theoretical, methodological, and mathematical technicalities are introduced promptly—for if they are not, the subject (at best, and if at all) will produce the kind of superficial, rule-of-thumb understanding evinced by my electrician friend whom I described in the preceding chapter. A more up-to-the-moment example, instead of the telephone (which Dewey used), is the computer (perhaps in the form of a smartphone); but from this starting point, one would not get far into modern science unless technicalities were introduced. (Indeed, the result might be the unfortunate maintenance of the bifurcation often expressed as the division between those who can *use* computers and those who are *used by* them!) I cannot resist laboring the point: Unless one has some command of the technicalities, how can one grasp the significance of, and nature of, the Einsteinian revolution, or the revolution in our knowledge of the subatomic world of quarks and strings, of the structure of the cosmos and the nature of black holes, or of the structure and functions of genes? In essence I am suggesting that Dewey was not paying sufficient attention to the issue of what constitutes *understanding* a science, for he was focusing on a different issue, namely, the social and therefore *human relevance* of science—but having this second focus does not excuse him from treating science adequately rather than superficially. It is relevant to note here that in the later decades of the twentieth century, in an effort to combat the scientific illiteracy of their nonscience majors, many colleges and universities developed courses popularly known as "physics for poets"—but these were (and are) generally of low repute due in large part to their avoidance of technicalities (and especially of mathematics).

To be fair, however, I need to point out that in his earlier work *The School and Society* Dewey does provide examples of introductory science lessons, but these are very brief, and are drawn from the University of Chicago elementary school. In D&E, while still having this elementary level as his prime focus, he also often seems to have high school and college-level courses in mind—although this is not specifically clarified for his readers. In all, however, it is quite noticeable that he does not give us a clear and precise account of what he considers a proper and nonsuperficial understanding of a specific branch of science to consist in.

I have already mentioned the development of "physics for poets" in the half century following Dewey's death, but many other things have taken place. For example, many colleges and universities have experimented with various types of distribution, or general education, requirements for undergraduates; these have been based on the principle that an educated person should at least have a nodding acquaintance with a branch each of science and mathematics or statistics, a branch of literature, something from history and/or philosophy, a social science, an area of art or drama or music, and possibly a foreign language. Dewey wanted the linkages between these domains to be made clear *within* the various subjects, whereas the dominant contemporary view seems to be that the linkages will be made—if at all—within the minds of the *individual learners* (which is not to deny that a few institutions have experimented with a more "Deweyan" approach). Other examples are the establishment of university departments of, and programs in, history and philosophy of science, and the appearance about twenty years ago of an international, interdisciplinary journal, *Science and Education*—one of the main aims of which has a clear Deweyan tone, namely, to promote "an understanding of the philosophical, cultural, economic, religious, psychological and ethical dimensions of modern science and the interplay of these factors in the history of science." (In the interest of full disclosure, I should mention that for many years I served on this journal's editorial board.) I should also draw attention to the massive curriculum development efforts that were mounted in the sciences in the UK and the USA, the catalyst for which was the launching by the Soviet Union of the first artificial satellite, *Sputnik*. These curricula (PSSC Physics is an outstanding example) were innovative attempts to give students a deep understanding of particular branches of science using many clever hands-on exercises.

Finally, no discussion of the science-humanities divide would be complete without mentioning the furor that arose within academic circles in 1959, about seven years after Dewey's death. It raged for many years, and I daresay embers can still be located today. The cause of the fuss was C. P. Snow's Rede Lecture, delivered over the BBC in the UK and subsequently published by Cambridge University Press in 1961 as *The Two Cultures and the Scientific Revolution*. A well-connected scientist who relatively late in life became a respected novelist, Snow argued that there were "two cultures."

> I believe the intellectual life of the whole of western society is increasingly being split in to two polar groups. . . . Literary intellectuals at one pole—at the other scientists, and as the most representative, the physical scientists. Between the two a gulf of mutual incomprehension—sometimes (particularly among the young) hostility and dislike, but most of all lack of understanding. (p. 4)

Adding to the furor was the fact that Snow did not mince his words; the title of his second chapter was "Intellectuals as Natural Luddites." The issue he raised, of course, was closely related to Dewey's concern in several chapters in D&E, but—and here I must be cautious as I have not studied this topic in depth for many years—Dewey's writings do not figure in the to-and-fro. I wonder why?

22

The Individual and the World

There are several "take-home" messages in this chapter, all of which have been met earlier in the book, and all of which are related to Dewey's sensitivity to false or misleading dualisms. First, Dewey discusses the tendency in Western thought to set up a dichotomy between the individual human being (referring to the mind and not the physical body) and the world; if indeed they are separate, self-sufficient entities, then the problem arises as to how one of these separate things (the mind) can come to know (or even to affect) the other. Second, according to Dewey's analysis, it follows that if the individual mind is separate from the world or from nature, then individual minds also must be separate from one another. This raises the problem of the precise nature of *social* life, and establishes the dualism between the individual mind and society. This in turn raises issues concerning the nature of individualism and intellectual freedom. Dewey, of course, advocates abandoning the dualisms that give rise to these problems. He puts the issues this way in the summary:

> The assertion that each individual's mind was complete in isolation from everything else . . . produced the epistemological problem: the question as to the possibility of any cognitive relationship of the individual to the world. In its practical phase, it generated the prob-

lem of the possibility of a purely individual consciousness acting on behalf of general or social interests.

To make his case, in the body of the chapter Dewey again resorts to using the genetic or historical approach, and the reaction is much the same reaction as the one produced by its use in the previous chapter. Those criticisms will not be revisited here, nor will I go through Dewey's arguments step-by-step. Instead I will cut to the chase and give my own gloss on the situation he is describing and critiquing. First, the mind-world dualism. Dewey touched on this several times earlier in D&E, and in my commentaries I pointed out that the dualism was related to the so-called spectator theory of knowledge (an epistemological position attacked by both William James and Dewey). The dualism set up a conundrum that has puzzled philosophers for eons—namely, how can a nonphysical entity (the mind) affect the course of events in the physical world? All of us, to give a simple illustration, have the strong sense that mental events (such as willing our arms to move) produce effects in the physical world (our arms normally start moving). The conundrum is that physical events require physical causes, and mental events by definition are not physical. In my comments on earlier chapters of D&E, I pointed out that Dewey argues that an "educational equivalent" of this dualism is that, when learning is taking place in schools, bodily activity is a distraction and must be repressed, for learning is an activity that involves the mind. (The old-fashioned schoolroom in which I was entrapped in a desk hopefully comes to mind.)

A simple but profound insight leads to the resolution of this dualism: Mind is not an entity that exists in a transcendent, nonphysical realm, but rather it is part of the physical world—it evolved within this world and was never separate from it. In chapter 11, I quoted William James as writing that mind "is in the game, and not a mere looker on," and I cited a passage from Dewey's *Quest for Certainty* as saying "mind is within the world as a part of the latter's own ongoing process." James had expounded this view, in sparkling prose, in chapter 3 of his *Talks to Teachers on Psychology* (1899):

> Man, we now have reason to believe, has been evolved from infrahuman ancestors, in whom pure reason hardly existed, if at all, and whose mind, so far as can have had any function, would appear to have been an organ for adapting their movements to the impressions received from the environment, so as to escape the better from destruction. Consciousness would [be] . . . useless unless it prompted to useful conduct, and inexplicable apart from that consideration.

The perspicuous reader might see a problem here for James and Dewey—namely, that they have not solved the problem at all! For they talk about "mind" existing in, and playing a role in, nature—without explaining how this is possible. However, although they certainly often refer to "mind" as if it were an entity, this was a matter of linguistic convenience. They explicitly regarded "it" as a capacity or ability possessed by certain biological organisms, the physical/biological basis for which is currently unknown.

So much for the mind-world dualism. In chapter 22 Dewey goes on to reconstruct the train of reasoning pursued by those who accepted this dualism. For these thinkers, mind is a non-physical entity that is "internal" to individuals and separate from the world. But if "the individual mind is a separate entity, complete in each person, and isolated from nature," then each mind would also be separate from other minds (for these "other minds" also are also individually "complete" and isolated). And thus another conundrum is born: Under these circumstances, what becomes of social motives for acting? From whence does knowledge of the social aspects of human existence arise? To get a "gut-level" feel for this issue, imagine a computer game in which hordes of sticklike figures are moving to and fro around the screen; they interact physically, for example, by colliding or swerving to avoid collisions, but they do not recognize each other as sources of intelligence—in short, at best they are self-centered humanoids. In this game, how would a sense of acting with the good of the (social) collective arise? How would it spread across the population to take root and eventually shape the behavior of all? In short, how would the unconnected mass become a society? Or as Dewey pithily phrased it in the middle of section 3 of chapter 22, "Given an egoistic consciousness, how can action which has regard for others take place?" Furthermore, it should be noted that in the opening chapter of D&E, Dewey clarified what he meant by a social community, an account that also serves to sharpen this problem:

> Persons do not become a society by living in physical proximity. . . . Individuals do not even compose a social group because they all work for a common end. The parts of a machine work with a maximum of cooperativeness for a common result, but they do not form a community. If, however, they were all cognizant of the common end and all interested in it so that they regulated their specific activity in view of it, then they would form a community.

Dewey was not the only early twentieth-century figure to tackle this conundrum, for social anthropologists also were concerned about it, as was Dewey's colleague and friend George Herbert Mead. The resolution of the problem closely parallels the resolution of the mind-world dualism discussed above. For upon reflection it becomes clear that the problem arises as a consequence of another dualism, namely, the mind-society dualism—and this can be resolved in the same fashion as was the previous dualism. In essence, the conundrum illustrated by the simple computer simulation assumes that individuals with minds (that is, individuals with intellectual capacity) came into existence first and came together later in some mysterious way to form a society. But the mystery disappears when it is realized that humans always were members of social groups—we evolved *within* such groups. Furthermore, each of us *becomes* an individual *within* a social group, drawing on social resources (language, symbol systems, knowledge, moral codes, and the like). Dewey writes early in section 2 of the chapter that "as a matter of fact every individual has grown up, and always must grow up, in a social medium." And he had made a related point almost twenty years earlier in his famous short essay "My Pedagogic Creed" (1897)—words I quoted in chapter 2—"if we eliminate the social factor from the child we are left only with an abstraction." And in the opening lines of section 2 of chapter 2 of D&E, he used the following example to make his point:

> We might as well try to imagine a business man doing business, buying and selling, all by himself, as to conceive it possible to define the activities of an individual in terms of his isolated actions.

The implications for intellectual freedom flow naturally from Dewey's analysis (and disposal) of the dualisms. Freedom is not freedom *from* society, but rather freedom *within* society—freedom to make use of its resources to further social ends. At the start of section 2 of chapter 22, Dewey says that "men were not actually engaged in the absurdity of striving to be free from connection with nature and one another. They were striving for greater freedom *in* nature and society." He elaborates in the second paragraph of section 3:

> There is tendency on the part of both the upholders and the opponents of freedom in school to identify it with absence of social direction, or, sometimes, with merely physical unconstraint of movement. But the essence of the demand for freedom is the need of conditions which will enable an individual to make his own special contribution to a group interest, and to partake of its activities in such ways that social guidance shall be a matter of his own mental attitude.

Two final matters require brief comment. First, in stressing that the development of the individual takes place within a social environment, Dewey was prescient, for this became an important theme in twentieth-century social science and developmental psychology. In 1915, of course, Dewey did not know of the work that was to come from Jean Piaget and Lev Vygotsky, but the different orientations of these two researchers are illustrative. Piaget tended to regard the developing human infant as a young, individual scientist, interacting with—and learning from—the environment in a solitary way. (Only a small fraction of Piaget's large corpus deals with the role of social factors in development.) Vygotsky, on the other hand, focused his attention on the ways in which young learners make vital use of social resources (this is captured in his famous concept of the "zone of proximal development"). Dewey, despite having some things in common with Piaget (both men were greatly influenced by evolutionary theory, and both saw the young learner as being both physically and mentally active), was—when push comes to shove—closer to Vygotsky.

Second, chapter 22 is worth mining carefully, for there are some phrases that are gems. I list only a few of my personal favorites, and leave it up to readers to produce their own: "thinking is as much a personal matter as is the digestion of food"; "there is no inherent opposition between working with others and working as an individual"; "the work was a piecemeal, a retail, business"; and "the self is not a separate mind building up knowledge anew on its own account."

23

Vocational Aspects of Education

It is vanishingly rare for a text in philosophy of education to contain any discussion—let alone a chapter-length treatment—of vocational education. For example, the term "vocational" does not even appear in the index to *Philosophy of Education* (Westview, 1995) by Nel Noddings, one of the leading contemporary volumes. The general modern feeling probably is that the topic is too narrow, and/or is too "unphilosophical." I must admit that although I vacillate, I tend to share this opinion. Perhaps Dewey shared it as well. For his aim in this chapter is not to elucidate the specific details of any particular vocational education program, and indeed his use of the term will strike some readers as nonstandard; rather, his intention is to continue his attack on the dualism between vocational education and liberal education, and thereby clarify the nature of *both* vocational and liberal studies. I used the expression "continue his attack" because, although the use of "vocational" in D&E is new, having only briefly appeared before, the dualism has appeared quite often in earlier chapters under different guises—intellectual versus practical, labor versus leisure, and body versus mind, to mention the most prominent. Dewey also uses the chapter to convey something of his attitude toward the age-old question of whether the school, as an institution within society, can aspire to reform the society of which it is part, or whether schooling itself first needs to be reformed by this society. (Although Dewey does not put it this way, it is a form of the chicken-and-egg conundrum—which comes first, the reformed chicken or the reformed egg?)

Before tackling the dualism, and the issue of reform, however, Dewey's use of "vocations," and the term he uses in earlier writings almost as a synonym, "occupations," requires some discussion. To make my first point in a graphic way, I bring an extremely simple parlor game—just devised by myself—to the attention of the flagging reader. Seek the cooperation of an unsuspecting colleague, and read the following passage from very early in the chapter to him or her:

> X means nothing but such a direction of life activities as renders them perceptibly significant to a person, because of the consequences they accomplish, and also useful to his associates.

Then ask what term is defined by the passage. X is used as a placeholder for "vocation" in the quotation. It is a safe bet that—if any answer is forthcoming—it will be way off target. Contrast this with the following definition of "vocation" taken from Webster:

> A particular occupation, business, profession, trade, or calling; a summons to, or predilection for, a particular activity or career.

I would not hazard a wager that your colleague would fail to identify the term being defined here, for this is a genuine reportive definition of "vocation."

Whatever Dewey was doing in the strange passage quoted above, he was not offering a definition—of any of the types recognized by philosophers. Rather than giving the Webster-like meaning of "vocation," at best the passage presents a theory or hypothesis about the *function* of a vocation—what role such a thing plays in the ongoing life of the person who has one. But as it stands, it is quite abstract, without grounding, and so we read on to see what the rest of the chapter makes of it.

My second point concerns Dewey's treatment of what he called "occupations" some decade and a half earlier in *The School and So-*

ciety (1900/1915) (S&S)—in which he devotes much of chapters 1 and 2 and all chapter 6 to them and their use in schools. In comparison with the treatment in D&E, this earlier work is sparkling and even engrossing. (The chapters of the original edition of S&S were written as public addresses, which perhaps explains some of their appeal.) "By occupation," he writes at the start of chapter 6,

> I mean a mode of activity on the part of the child which reproduces, or runs parallel to, some form of work carried on in social life. . . . As an occupation it is active or motor; it finds expression through the physical organs—the eyes, hands, etc. But it also involves continual observation of materials, and continual planning and reflection, in order that the practical or executive side may be successfully carried on.

As such, Dewey stresses, an occupation must be carefully distinguished from work that trains for a trade. It differs, he continues, because "its end is in itself . . . not in external utility." I put forth the following example to clarify what Dewey evidently intends here: if the activity of weaving is used in school to sensitize students to the historical importance of wool cloth, and its advantages and disadvantages compared with cotton, and so forth, then it is an "occupation" with genuine educational value; if, however, weaving is taught as a marketable skill—as a prospective way of earning a living—it is not what he would call an "occupation," but rather is "learning a trade." Much of what he says about occupations here and elsewhere in S&S parallels the points he makes in his later discussion of vocations in D&E; although the two are not exactly the same in meaning, he sometimes uses them as synonyms. So first, then, what are these mysterious "occupations"?

To answer this, we must go back to the past, but this time not to the days of Plato, but to a time in the United States "when the household was practically the center in which were carried on . . . all the typical forms of industrial occupation," that is, to the days of Dewey's own childhood in pre– and post–Civil War Vermont—of which he seems to have had vivid (if slightly romanticized) memories. Members of a family were generally acquainted with the making of clothes, the gathering of food, the husbandry of animals, the forging of metal, the elements of carpentry, the preparation of candles, and so forth—all of which were occupations vital to sustaining life, and all of which had an important social aspect. (I have a friend who, several decades ago—that is, well over a century later than the time Dewey was writing about—moved to northern Michigan, where the entire rural community joined together on several occasions to prepare for the rigors of winter. The first inkling he had of this was when he was invited to a gathering devoted to the "making of firewood"—that is, to the gathering and cutting of firewood.) Dewey wrote in chapter 1 of S&S:

> We cannot overlook the factors of discipline and of character-building involved in this kind of life: training in habits of order and of industry, and in the idea of responsibility, of obligation to do something, to produce something, in the world. There was always something that really needed to be done, and a real necessity that each member of the household should do his own part faithfully and in cooperation with others. . . . The educative forces of the domestic spinning and weaving, of the sawmill, the gristmill, the cooper shop, and the blacksmith forge, were continuously operative.

Occupations, then, were a vital part of family—and community—life in an age that to a great extent is a fading memory. Why introduce them into the schools of today? Here Dewey has a brilliant insight. Over the course of time, as society has changed with the introduction of new industrial and manufacturing processes, those practices of yesteryear have been gradually abandoned—and lost along with them have been the "affordances" they offered for the acquisition of vital, really vital, social and personal skills and attitudes. Because it is essential that youngsters acquire these, the school must pick up the slack; furthermore, these social and personal skills and attitudes need to be passed on in an environment similar to the one in which they were effectively transmitted in the past. In the first chapter of S&S, there are many passages where, with some rhetorical flair, Dewey makes these points. For example,

> We must conceive of work in wood and metal, of weaving, sewing, and cooking, as methods of living and learning. . . . We must conceive of them in their social significance, as types of the processes by which society keeps itself going, as agencies for bringing home to the child some of the primal necessities of community life. . . . Upon the ethical side, the tragic weakness of the present school is that it endeavors to prepare future members of the social order in a medium in which the conditions of the social spirit are eminently wanting.

What will be the upshot if the needed corrective changes are made in schooling?

> When the school introduces and trains each child of society into membership within such a little community, saturating him with the spirit of service, and providing him with the instruments of effective self-direction, we shall have the deepest and best guaranty of a larger society which is worthy, lovely, and harmonious.

In other words, the reformed school egg will produce the reformed society chicken.

It may seem as if this side excursion to contemplate "occupations" in S&S has taken us a long way from "vocations," but in fact we have covered some important terrain. So in chapter 23 of D&E, we meet some now familiar points. First, the various "philosophical dualisms" are "deeply entangled" with the "whole subject of vocational education." Second, Dewey states that we need to "avoid the impression that an education which centers about it [vocational education] is narrowly practical, if not merely pecuniary" (for if it has this narrow focus it is training for a trade, and is not broadly *educational*.) These extracts were taken from the second paragraph of the chapter, where on one occasion Dewey uses "occupation" when he discusses "vocation." At the start of the next paragraph he writes:

> We must avoid not only limitation of conception of vocation to the occupations where immediately tangible commodities are produced,

> but also the notion that vocations are distributed in an exclusive way, one and only one to each person. . . . No one is just an artist and nothing else, and in so far as one approximates that condition, he is so much the less developed human being; he is a kind of monstrosity. He must, at some period of his life, be a member of a family; he must have friends and companions. . . . He has a business career. He is a member of some organized political unit, and so on. We naturally *name* his vocation from that one of the callings which distinguishes him.

Among other things, this passage clarifies (or perhaps, partially clarifies) Dewey's usage of "occupations" and "vocation": a person engages in many occupations, but the one that "distinguishes" him or her is the vocation of that individual. Webster might regard this as a near miss.

Dewey goes on to stress that education "through occupations" combines "within itself more of the factors conducive to learning than any other method." It calls instincts and habits into play, it "appeals to thought," it requires "observation and ingenuity," and so on. He repeats and then amplifies this thought in the fourth paragraph of section 2 (again using "occupation" instead of "vocation"):

> The only adequate training *for* occupations is training *through* occupations. The principle stated earlier in this book (see Chapter VI) that the educative process is its own end, and that the only sufficient preparation for later responsibilities comes by making the most of immediately present life, applies in full force to the vocational phases of education. The dominant vocation of all human beings at all times is living—intellectual and moral growth. . . . To predetermine some future occupation for which education is to be a strict preparation is to injure the possibilities of present development and thereby to reduce the adequacy of preparation for a future right employment.

Near the end of the chapter, Dewey makes the point that the occupations of the past (presumably those he had discussed in S&S) provided rich educational opportunities, and the task for the present is to similarly capitalize on the rich potentialities within contemporary industry and manufacturing—but without making the school "an adjunct of manufacture and commerce," which he acknowledged to be a problem "not of easy solution." (From the perspective of a century later, his words were perhaps a tad too soft, for the dominant tendency in much current educational policy talk is to treat education as the key to national economic development, and that only.) Dewey has a broader, and I daresay nobler, vision—and one that is remarkably true to his position earlier in S&S:

> The key to the present educational situation lies in a gradual reconstruction of school materials and methods so as to utilize various forms of occupations typifying social callings, and to bring out their intellectual and moral content. This transformation . . . signifies a society in which every person shall be occupied in something which makes the lives of others better worth living.

24

Philosophy of Education

The subtitle of D&E, at this stage possibly long-forgotten by many readers, proclaims the volume to be "an introduction to the philosophy of education." In this third-from-last chapter the expectation set by the subtitle is finally cashed in. Some readers—like Molière's character who discovered that he had been speaking prose all his life—will be delighted to learn that, according to Dewey, they have been engaged with philosophy of education all the while they have been working through the book. But if you are one of this number, keep the lid on your cup of joy—for Dewey's view of the domain of philosophy of education is contested, and certainly is different from several of the views that jostle for supremacy in our contemporary world.

The chapter opens with a section that summarizes the content of the previous twenty-three chapters, bringing out the links between them and revealing the philosophical issues "involved" in them. It is the kind of summary often met in the introductory chapter in scholarly volumes, particularly in edited collections. In my view, Dewey's placement of the summaries near the end rather than at the beginning of the book is far superior, for at the outset the reader is partially (or wholly) ignorant, and therefore the summaries mean nothing—it is only after one has worked through the material that one can comprehend the précis. But, of course, an issue arises here: How accurate are Dewey's summaries? Has he in fact accomplished what he claims to have achieved? I will leave this general issue for the reader to decide, for having reached this advanced stage in D&E, you will no doubt have your own well-founded judgment about what has been done.

However, one needs to proceed to judgment with caution. Dewey—like many scholars, including yours truly—occasionally sees his own work through rose-colored glasses, and makes claims about his previous work that are not indubitably substantiated. (I confess to my having written, on occasion, statements along the lines of "as I have previously established . . . ," when it turns out that in fact I have established no such thing.) One example from the first section of chapter 24 will suffice; it may—or may not—be a picayune point, but as a philosopher it is my bent to note slips like this on the part of others in my guild. In the third paragraph, Dewey writes as follows:

> The general discussion was then specified by application to social groups which are intentionally progressive, and which aim at a greater variety of mutually shared interests. . . . Such societies were found to be democratic in quality, because of the greater freedom allowed to the constituent members.

I challenge Dewey's claim (an important one, in my view) that these societies were *found* to be democratic, for the fact is that he *defines* "democracy" in terms of the possession of such features. The broader moral here is that before one buys into any philosopher's position (including the one outlined in this companion), it is wise to bear in mind the old saying *caveat emptor!*

In his summary of the previous chapters, Dewey makes the point that the democratic "criterion" has faced "limitations" with respect to its "actual realization"; and these limitations can be traced to the false dualisms that abound. He suggests several ways to combat these, of which two stand out in my judgement. The first is by laying emphasis on the evolutionary conception of mind; Dewey phrases the point this way:

> Underlying these various separations [dualisms] we found the fundamental assumption to be an isolation of mind from activity involving physical conditions, bodily organs, material appliances, and natural objects. *Consequently, there was indicated a philosophy which recognizes the origin, place, and function of mind in an activity which controls the environment.* [Italics added.]

The second way forward is by recognizing the "dependence of the growth of mind upon participation in conjoint activities having a common purpose"—in other words, by recognizing that mind develops in, and operates in, a social setting.

And so we arrive at the long second section, devoted to expounding Dewey's view of the "nature of philosophy." He opens his account by restating his view that the contents of philosophy—the problems or subject matter with which it deals—"originate in the conflicts and difficulties of social life." This position is explained lucidly, and in more depth, in *Reconstruction in Philosophy*, but in neither place does he recognize that once systems of thought arise, they generate many of their serious problems from within. To borrow a term used by Israel Scheffler to describe the developmental trajectory of science, the development of philosophy is to an important degree *autonomous*. Consider, by way of analogy, how number systems—which we may say evolved to aid human societies with real-world problems such as commercial transactions and the surveying of land—soon generated "internal" problems that to a considerable extent drove their development: real versus unreal numbers, the existence of infinitesimals, how to conceptualize infinite series, Goldbach's conjecture, and the like. This is why focusing the teaching of a subject on its social usages, which of course is a Deweyan mantra, may not be an adequate way of leading students to more than a superficial understanding of it.

It seems as if Dewey was misled here by his use of the so-called genetic method (a practice that he specifically acknowledges and explains in the early pages of *Reconstruction*). As pointed out several times earlier in this companion, the method of tracing the origin of some entity or practice, and stressing the function that it evolved to carry out, is used a number of times in D&E. But unless one is extremely careful, its use can lead one to commit a form of the "genetic fallacy" whereby the original function of the entity or practice is taken to be the *only* function it can have; in other words, one can be blinded to the fact that once developed, this entity or practice can open up, and take on, new functions. Thus, even if philosophy did originate to carry out the social purposes Dewey suggests, it does not follow that now that it has been developed, it must not take on new functions and face new problems that have opened up. (Biological evolution provides many examples of features that evolved within a species to carry out one function and later shed that function to carry out new ones; as discussed earlier, the evolution of the human hand is perhaps a good example of this.)

But Dewey moves on, and so must we. The next point he makes is that "whenever philosophy has been taken seriously," it has been regarded as "achieving a wisdom which would influence the conduct of life." Certainly examples can be found to illustrate this, and undoubtedly questions like the following have played an important role in philosophical discourse: How should I live? What is it to lead a moral life? What is my duty to the country of which I am a citizen? Do the bonds of friendship ever outweigh the duties of citizenship? But surely, without elaborate "special pleading," it is difficult to maintain that *all* genuine philosophy has this "outlook on life." Are not, for example, the following issues genuinely philosophical in nature—the problem of induction, methodological individualism versus collectivism, internal versus external relations, the problem of indexicals, the underdetermination of theory by evidence, the Gettier problem, the "grue" paradox, Zeno's paradox? It is difficult to see how having a well-thought-out position with regard to indexicals* will allow one to lead a happier and more fulfilling life, or to be a better citizen. If only!

* Indexicals are words such as "I," "we," "you," and "here" that change reference when the speaker or the context changes; they are the source of technical problems in the philosophy of language.

Dewey continues his exposition by asserting that this "intimate connection of philosophy with an outlook upon life" is what differentiates philosophy from science. For science tells us about particular facts and laws, and this information may often suggest things to do and not to do, but when science "denotes" not just specific things to do but puts forward "a *general attitude*" toward the world, "it merges into philosophy." He writes:

> When we ask what *sort* of permanent disposition of action toward the world the scientific disclosures exact of us we are raising a philosophic question. . . . Knowledge, grounded knowledge, is science. . . . Philosophy is thinking what the known demands of us—what responsive attitude it exacts.

This is a noble, "generative" view of the function of philosophy. Dewey elaborates it a tad further when he says that when conflicts arise between the "various interests" in life—for example, between the scientific and religious interests, or between the economic and aesthetic—then this is a stimulus to discover a more comprehensive view, and therein lies the role of philosophy.

Here several comments are in order. First, Dewey's description of the role of philosophy is quite abstract—he needs to "unpack" statements like "thinking what the known demands of us" or having "a general attitude toward the world" by, perhaps, walking us carefully through an example or two in order to clarify what he is suggesting. But as it stands, he fails to give us this concrete understanding. The nearest he comes to being specific is when he refers to the various and often conflicting interests in life, and claims that it is the role of philosophy to bring peace by finding a "more comprehensive view." This is what I referred to above as a "generative" view, and it has a distinctly Hegelian ring to it.

In chapter 10 of this companion, I discussed Dewey's attachment to Hegelian philosophy, and his use of the famous "dialectical method" to dispose of, or to disarm, dualisms that masked the organic interrelatedness that was pervasive in the world. In sum, a *thesis* about some aspect of the world would "generate" an opposing *antithesis*, thus establishing a dualism. The conflict or tension between these "poles" could be resolved by formulating a *synthesis* that either combined the best of both the opposing positions, or that presented a new way of conceptualizing matters that resolved the conflict and pointed the way forward. (The earlier discussion in chapters 9 and 10 contains some examples of Dewey's use of this Hegelian procedure.) It is arguable that this very same pattern lies just beneath the surface of Dewey's position here in chapter 24—namely, that the role of philosophy is to formulate a "more comprehensive view" (that is, a synthesis) that resolves the conflict between the "various interests in life," which are in essence the poles of one or another dualism. Herman Harrell Horne, in his companion to D&E, makes the same point. Dewey, he writes, "holds that philosophy seeks to comprehend and unify a conflict of interests. The method is Hegel's." But Horne points out that there is a difference. Hegel applies the method to all phases of reality, while "Dewey applies his only to social struggles" (p. 471).

Dewey's "vision" (if that is what it is) faces the problem that in contemporary society there are many folk—outside the realm of philosophy—who are socially empowered to put forward "comprehensive views" (especially at election time!); and concomitantly, there are many within the field of philosophy who are extremely reluctant to take on this generative responsibility on the grounds that their discipline does not bestow on them the appropriate range of skills and expertise. (For example, how does a philosopher's skill at dealing with indexicals and other issues in philosophy of language equip him or her to develop "comprehensive views" that resolve dualisms? And the same might be asked of a philosopher of education whose recent work focuses on technical issues in the realm of educational research design.) Dewey evidently felt competent to do this generative work, and indeed he became a well-known "public intellectual" who spoke out sensibly on the great social issues of his day—but surely he was overreaching to suggest that the function of the whole field of philosophy should be based on his own personal talents and predilections.

This leads to a second comment about Dewey's conception of philosophy and philosophy of education. It is markedly different from accounts that have been given in more recent times—with an important proviso. Dewey and I both are using "philosophy" and "philosopher" in what might be called their technical senses. There is, however, a nontechnical, everyday usage wherein any individual who thinks on an abstract or general level about deep issues can be said to be doing philosophy. Such individuals can often be seen at work on cable television, and they often advance "comprehensive views" in order to solve pressing social problems. Clearly, however, D&E—conceived as an introduction to the field of philosophy of education—was considering only the technical sense of the key term.

Let's put the proviso aside, then, and note that one influential account of the nature of philosophy—and perforce of philosophy of education—that is at odds with Dewey's account appears in Ludwig Wittgenstein's *Philosophical Investigations*, first published in 1953 shortly after Dewey's death. Wittgenstein wrote, in characteristic style, "What is your aim in philosophy?—To show the fly the way out of the fly-bottle" (p. 309). What Wittgenstein was suggesting here (he rarely said things directly, his style being designed to get his readers to philosophize along with him) was that the role of philosophy was to help us escape from hopeless entanglement in problems that were not genuine ones about the world, but rather were artifacts arising from the misuse of ordinary language. Philosophy did not change the world (at least not directly), but changed how we thought and wrote about it. This approach became known as "ordinary language analysis," and it dominated philosophy of education in the English-speaking world for three decades or so beginning around 1960, and its influence is still considerable (and it even had an impact on the author of your companion). Over this period a large amount of work appeared that aimed to clarify the "logic" (conditions for the proper use) of educational concepts such as learning, teaching, indoctrination, autonomy, punishment, rationality, creativity—and of course, the concept of education itself.

Another approach has been to view philosophy of education as a branch of philosophy analogous, in its aims and the kinds of contributions it makes, to branches of the discipline such as philosophy of science and philosophy of history; and philosophy of education is also seen here as having the same kind of relation to the parent educational disciplines as those other branches of philosophy have to theirs. Philosophers of science, in this example, attempt to clarify the nature of scientific explanation and prediction by studying what physical and biological scientists themselves regard as exemplary cases, they analyze the structure of scientific theories, they study notions of causation—and methods of determining causes—as these appear in scientific practice, they try to ascertain the conditions under which scientists will regard a hypothesis as having been refuted, and so on. Analogously, according to this account of the field, philosophers of education ought to study the nature of educational theories, the adequacy of research designs, the issue of causation when human phenomena are the object of study, the role of value judgments in educational discourse, the conceptions of educational equity that appear in educational policy debates, and so on. And just as much work in philosophy of science is a contribution to philosophy, so is (or should be) work done in philosophy of education.

There are several other approaches to philosophy of education, and the interested reader can find them outlined in a number of reference works, including the lengthy entry "Philosophy of Education"—coauthored by myself—in the online *Stanford Encyclopedia of Philosophy*. Enough has been written here, however, to indicate some ways in which the contemporary field differs from Dewey's vision of a century ago. But it also needs to be acknowledged that the contemporary scene is complex; and there is some work in the field that can be argued is closer in spirit to Dewey than the account I have given above suggests. Thus the text by Nel Noddings that I mentioned earlier, *Philosophy of Education* (1995), correctly points out that

> despite the dominant analytical view of twentieth-century philosophy, philosophers have sometimes created theories, and today many philosophers engage in constructive work. They introduce new language and suggest powerful alternatives to the standard uses of language. Some now even draw heavily on literature and empirical

> data in the form of teaching narratives to make points that cannot be made in the traditional style of argumentation. (pp. 1–2)

But Noddings continues with an important rider: "Whether this work is properly called philosophy is part of an exciting contemporary debate." In the spirit of full disclosure, I must admit that I have taken the position in this debate that one has to be extremely charitable in order to judge that much of this new work falls within the hallowed walls of philosophy.

Two issues that arise in the long second section of chapter 24 in D&E remain to be discussed. The first of these concerns the point Dewey emphasizes in the eighth paragraph before the section's end. "The student of philosophy 'in itself,'" he writes,

> is always in danger of taking it as so much nimble or severe intellectual exercise—as something said by philosophers and concerning them alone. But . . . If a theory makes no difference in educational endeavor, it must be artificial.

And a little later he adds that if philosophy is to avoid being "arbitrary dogma," it must "take effect in conduct." It is not entirely surprising that Dewey held this view, for it can be argued that in doing so he was being true to one of the basic tenets of pragmatism, namely, that the function of ideas—including philosophical ideas—is to guide action.

However, there is an interesting side effect. Dewey's words here seem to have fostered—or perhaps "fueled" is a better term—an approach to teaching philosophy of education that has long since been debunked. Often referred to as the "isms" approach, this held that various philosophical schools or "isms"—realism, idealism, Thomism, pragmatism, for example—should be explained to the student (usually a student teacher), along with their differing educational "implications" (they must have such implications, if Dewey's analysis is correct, for otherwise these positions would be artificial). The student would then be able to decide personally which approach to adopt in his or her teaching. The problem is, of course, that the link between an "ism" and the real world is far from straightforward (if it exists at all), yet it is hard to say that these "isms" are merely artificial. In fact, they are well-developed philosophical positions that answer in their own ways deep philosophical questions.

An example is in order here. With some hesitancy I draw on an instance from my own teaching of an introductory course in philosophy of education about four decades ago; my reluctance stems from the fact that (perhaps mercifully) the mists of time have somewhat clouded my memory of some of the relevant details. But lack of specificity should never be allowed to interfere with a good story! I had discovered the existence of a series of short instructional films, each one of which was devoted to a particular philosophical "ism" and its (so-called) educational implications. With a degree of malicious delight, I screened two of these for my class—those on "realism" and "idealism," for these made a nice contrast. The films had the same format—each started with a short lecture lasting about ten minutes from a philosopher about the relevant philosophical "ism"; this was followed by a scene shot in a real school classroom where a teacher of the relevant philosophical persuasion was at work. It was remarkable how different these two teachers were. The realist almost shouted his points to the class; he stamped about the classroom as he talked, intermittently hammering on the front desk and the chalkboard to emphasize his points—for obviously he harbored no doubts about the reality of these objects. In marked contrast, the idealist teacher was a timid fellow; he was careful not to move or to touch anything, and clearly was in mortal fear of sinking through the floorboards or plunging his arm through the chalkboard—for these were not realities but mere "ideas" that were, as Shakespeare's Prospero put it, "such stuff as dreams are made on." My students agreed with me that, under the circumstances, we would be foolish not to opt for the lifestyle of the realist! But, of course, the simple fact of the matter is that one cannot tell by observing people's behavior who is a philosophical realist and who is an idealist—for these are philosophical and not empirical theories. Dewey was too good a philosopher not to understand all of this, so one wishes that he had taken more care in elucidating his position.

It is important to note that Dewey had more than three decades of work ahead of him after the publication of D&E, so one must not take his position here as his very last word on the nature of philosophy. Indeed, there is evidence that during this latter period Dewey struggled to produce an account of the "philosopher's task" that he regarded as satisfactory. Philip Jackson, for example, wrote a book-length study of the various reformulations Dewey produced, between 1925 and the time of his death in 1952, of the introductory chapter of *Experience and Nature*—a chapter titled "Experience and Philosophic Method." What drove the constant revisions of this introduction, Jackson points out, was "a formidable old problem" that had plagued Dewey since the start of his professional career—namely, "the question of how philosophers should go about their work" (*John Dewey and the Philosopher's Task* [2002], p. xviii).

Finally, we come to probably the most famous point Dewey made about the relation between philosophy and education. In the last few pages of section 2, he asserts that "philosophy may even be defined *as the general theory of education*." But he also gives some alternative formulations of what evidently is the same general view: "Education is the laboratory in which philosophic distinctions become concrete and are tested." And then a few paragraphs later he repeats his basic thought, "The most penetrating definition of philosophy which can be given is, then, that it is the theory of education in its most general phases." In the summary a paragraph or so later he reiterates that

> philosophic thinking has for its differentia the fact that the uncertainties with which it deals are found in widespread social conditions and aims, consisting in a conflict of organized interests and institutional claims.

On the face of it, this is an analysis of major importance—although it remains a tad mysterious. So it is surprising that Dewey does not revisit it in later books where he has lengthy discussions of the nature of philosophy, such as *Reconstruction in Philosophy* and *Experience and Nature*. Mystery upon mystery!

I must admit to having mixed feelings about Dewey's thesis.

If taken as a generalization about the nature of all philosophy, and about the field's relation to education, then—as I hope I have made clear in the preceding discussion in this chapter and also earlier—I regard it as overblown and mistaken; but when it is applied to some specific instances, I find Dewey's analysis to be extremely revealing. For example, the body-mind dualism, discussed in chapter 11, certainly seems related to the social and educational practice of treating learning as a mental phenomenon in which bodily activity is seen as an interfering factor that needs to be suppressed. (Which came first, the practice of suppressing bodily activity while learning was taking place, or the dualism that served as the "philosophical underpinning" of this practice, is of course a moot point.) And it does seem plausible that the theory that explains the contemporary educational practice of engaging students both mentally and physically in their learning is the philosophical theory that resolves the body-mind dualism in the way discussed earlier. So in this particular case, the philosophical theory can be considered to be, at an abstract or general level, the theory that undergirds this aspect of education. And it is even more plausible to argue that educational practice is the arena ("laboratory" if you will) in which the (mistaken) philosophical distinction between mind and body "becomes concrete" and is "tested"—and of course in which it has been found wanting!

Obviously there is a lot more to puzzle over here, but I will let the last word go to Martin Dworkin, editor of *Dewey on Education: Selections*, a collection of extracts from Dewey's writings on education published in 1959, the centenary of Dewey's birth. In his introductory essay, Dworkin wrote:

> His conception of the discipline of philosophy as the generalization of educational theory appealed directly to a hallowed American reluctance to theorize. Here seemed to be a way to philosophize by *doing*, rather than by thinking only. . . . The educator would be the philosopher thinking aloud, and his "thoughts" would be the actual experiences of the children in the schools. (p. 14)

25

Theories of Knowledge

As Dewey acknowledges in the opening sentence of this chapter, a number of "theories of knowing" have been discussed in earlier parts of D&E; the purpose here is to revisit them on a more philosophical plane, and to bring out (or reemphasize) the main features of Dewey's own position. Thus we meet some now familiar entities—dualisms, spectator theories, "educational precipitates," the scientific method, and others. Dewey disposes of those that are defective, and embraces the good, without blinking an eye—making this chapter a useful reminder of many of the themes of the preceding twenty-four. Once again, however, it is a case of caveat emptor, for Dewey may well have been somewhat unrealistic about what his earlier discussions had *established* versus what they only *asserted*.

The chapter has two sections; the main theme in the first is that theories of knowing that are dualistic are deficient, for they deny continuity; the scientific method of knowing, however, does not do this. The second section places stress on the theme that although an item of knowledge may have originated in the past, its function lies in the future—in guiding our future interactions with our environment so that our problem-solving activities are successful. Here, too, the scientific method is the superior approach to gaining knowledge. So to start at the beginning . . .

Dewey crams a lot into the opening paragraph. He reminds his readers that the divisions, or dualisms, embodied in many theories of knowledge reflect divisions or barriers within society—between class and class, men and women, rich and poor, rulers and the ruled. These barriers "mean" an "absence of fluent and free intercourse" between the constituents of the opposing poles of the dualism; and this is what Dewey also means when he refers to a denial of continuity. Dewey is mistaken, I believe, to suppose that he had *established* such a tight connection between philosophical positions and social divisions or hierarchies. It certainly is an interesting thesis (one that is reminiscent of a hallmark position of Karl Marx), and it has some credibility, but establishing it as fact requires much more detailed and careful argument than Dewey has given it here. Horne, too, is dubious about Dewey's thesis, and writes appositely that "from divisions in society to dualism in epistemology is a far cry. It suggests that philosophy is another expression of the class struggle, that thought, arising in the strife of parties, can not rise above the strife" (p. 484). Indeed, Horne identifies several historical cases that seem to counter Dewey's account.

But let's continue the discussion of what precisely Dewey said about dualisms: In various of his writings, Dewey has offered two reasons why the setting up of these dualistic divisions is a mistake; indeed, there is a relevant discussion earlier in D&E, in chapter 10, that I draw on here. First, a dualism establishes a situation in which two different sets of life experience are set in opposition—we are forced, by the form of the dualism, to pick one or the other pole, when we really stand to gain by accepting the experiences of those at both. And under some circumstances (Dewey is a tad vague about this in the first paragraph of chapter 25), a dualism can lead to a flight from reality and into some transcendental realm (that is, a realm transcending the physical world, a realm not directly open to experience except perhaps when one is in a condition favorable to having mystical or religious experiences).

Second, Dewey thinks it generally is a philosophical mistake to establish a dualism, for while the drawing of such a distinction might have some usefulness for the purposes of thought, it is dangerous because it is also likely to be reified—it can tempt one to take this distinction in thought as marking a real division in the world. This is a mistake, because the world does not consist of separate parts that merely interact; rather it is continuous, made up (as Hegelians put it) of internally related "parts," that is, of holistically or organically interdependent "parts" that mutually support and influence each other, and which cannot in practice be meaningfully cast asunder. (Indeed the term "parts" itself is misleading, for it implies real divisions, not continuity.)

In the body of the first section of chapter 25, Dewey briefly deals with several dualisms that have had deleterious consequences; and then, near the end of this section, he enters into a long discussion of three developments (he calls them "forces") in the modern world that have established the fact of continuity beyond all reasonable doubt—that "tend to make the untenability of this [dualistic] conception obvious and to replace it by the idea of continuity." His choice of these three particular "forces" indicates that by 1916 Dewey was relying on biological/naturalistic arguments, rather than Hegelian metaphysical ones, although both of these lines of proceeding lead in the same direction.

The first of the three developments Dewey draws attention to is advances in physiology and psychology; "no one," he says,

> who has realized the full force of the facts of the connection of knowing with the nervous system and of the nervous system with the readjusting of activity continuously to meet new conditions, will doubt that knowing has to do with reorganizing activity, instead of being something isolated from all activity, complete on its own account.

The second is the development of evolutionary biology, the philosophical significance of which "lies precisely in its emphasis upon continuity of simpler and more complex organic forms until we reach man." And the third is the "development of the experimental method as the method of getting knowledge and of making sure it *is* knowledge, and not mere opinion." He elaborates on this factor for almost a page, in the course of which he makes a point that later became associated with the philosopher of science Karl Popper:

> The scientific experimental method is . . . a trial of ideas; hence even when practically—or immediately—unsuccessful, it is intellectual, fruitful; for we learn from our failures when our endeavors are seriously thoughtful.

Popper made the point in a more colorful way by comparing a scientist and an amoeba:

> The scientist's trials and errors consist of hypotheses. He formulates them in words. . . . He can then try to find flaws in any one of these hypotheses, by criticizing it, and by testing it experimentally. . . . If the hypothesis does not stand up to these criticisms and to these tests at least as well as its competitors, it will be eliminated. It is different with . . . the amoeba. Here there is no critical attitude, and so it happens more often than not that natural selection eliminates a mistaken hypothesis or expectation by eliminating those organisms which hold it. . . . So we can say that the critical or rational method consists in letting our hypotheses die in our stead. (*Objective Knowledge* [OUP, 1972], pp. 247–48)

It is fairly clear how the first two of these three factors help undergird the "idea of continuity"; however, the link between this idea and the scientific method might at first sight require further explication. But in the end the connection is relatively straightforward: The scientific method treats knowing as a process that occurs *within* the world; the knower manipulates objects and situations to determine the outcome, and is able to test the hypotheses that had been formulated about that situation. The knower here is part of the world—continuous with it, a participant in it, and by no means a spectator of it. This contrasts markedly with other classic theories of knowing. In the theories of Plato and others, the knower has to (mentally or intellectually) enter a transcendental realm that is separate and in a sense "above" the physical realm in order to contemplate the "Forms" or the "Absolute" or whatever; or else the knower has to draw on a nonphysical, nonnaturalistic faculty of reason (the belief in which is a consequence of setting up a dualism between mind and body). Both these alternatives embody denials of continuity, for they establish a discontinuity between the knower and the world.

The first section ends with a brief lay sermon, to which I personally add an "amen":

> But every advance in the influence of the experimental method is sure to aid in outlawing the literary, dialectic, and authoritative methods of forming beliefs which have governed the schools of the past. . . . In time the theory of knowing must be derived from the practice which is most successful in making knowledge.

Dewey has often been criticized for holding this belief, which—it is said—is indicative of his "scientism." I am dubious about this charge; surely it is sensible to argue that if we wish to improve a particular practice (ice-skating, to take an example with which I am completely unfamiliar), we would be well advised to study an expert in this practice (or somebody with enough skills to be an effective coach). As with skating, so with knowledge making, if Dewey is scientistic, it seems as if he also must be ice-skating-istic. (But the thought intervenes—perhaps I'm being scientistic in thinking that this argument is convincing!) It is time, however, to hasten to the second section of chapter 25.

Immediately we run into an opening paragraph that, like the opener in the previous section, packs in a great deal. Dewey begins by listing a number of "systems of philosophy" that have their own "conceptions of the method of knowing"—all of which "deviate" from the method, the scientific method of course, that has "proved most effective in achieving knowledge." Considering how these philosophies deviate from the scientific method helps clarify the role that genuine knowledge plays in the ongoing "stream of experience" (to modify a famous expression of William James's). Dewey's conclusion, "in brief," is that "the function of knowledge is to make one experience freely available in other experiences." The next sentence draws a contrast between action inspired by knowledge and action that is habitual, an issue Dewey elaborates in the remainder of this long paragraph.

On a first reading (and to be honest, on a second and a third as well) this is somewhat murky. One wonders why Dewey did not spell out in more "user-friendly" terms the points he was endeavoring to make here. Modestly, I will step into the breach to offer the following translation: The scientific method involves accepting—on the basis of past experience—certain items of knowledge (certain "knowledge claims") as being well warranted, and treating them as resources that are available for use in shaping future experience (i.e., future intervention in the world). If these knowledge claims lead to success, well and good; if not, we learn from our mistakes, and modify our putative knowledge, and try again. Thus our bodies of knowledge, our warranted knowledge claims, serve to "make [the fruits of] one experience freely available in other experiences." Other knowledge-producing philosophies, however, have different ways of dealing with experience. For example, if the traditional beliefs we hold come into conflict with what seems to be indicated by experience, in effect some philosophies say "so much the worse for experience," and insist that the prior beliefs must be maintained; the new, troublesome experience must be discounted as being either impious or less authoritative than reason or tradition. So, according to an example from an earlier chapter, there is no point in peering down Galileo's telescope, for reason tells us what the facts of the matter are, and if telescopic observation appears to indicate something different, then it simply is mistaken! And if there is no conflict, the observation is merely confirming the obvious! Ergo, telescopic observation is a waste of time.

Dewey's introduction of "habit" at this point should now be clear. Habits also make the products of past experience available for future guidance, and do so in a manner which, of course, is often quite advantageous. (Earlier in D&E Dewey wrote favorably about "intelligent habits.") But patterns of action that are the product of habit are more inflexible, less adaptable, than patterns of action that are the direct result of the application of knowledge. Habit, in short, "does not make allowance for change of conditions, for novelty."

The remainder of section 2 elaborates on these themes, and it ends with a nice summary (nicer than the summary that follows it):

> The theory of the method of knowing which is advanced in these pages may be termed pragmatic. Its essential feature is to maintain the continuity of knowing with an activity which purposely modifies the environment. . . . Knowledge is not just something which we are now conscious of, but consists of the dispositions we consciously use in understanding what now happens.

Dewey spoils this summary by using the far from clear (and far from usual) expression which states that knowing is "continuous with" activity that modifies the environment. Surely his point throughout has been that knowing *is* (or essentially involves) such activity, not that it is somehow "continuous" with it. (Dining is not "continuous" with eating, as if it were even faintly possible to separate the two; dining involves eating, or in other words, eating is part of what it means to dine. Certainly when you are finished dining, you are finished eating, but this is not because the two are linked by a principle of continuity—they are linked by virtue of their meanings!)

It is a shame to end discussion of this interesting chapter on yet another negative note, but I am impelled to point out the unfortunate second paragraph of section 2 where Dewey is quite disparaging about "savages." It is not simply that sensitivity to derogatory language has increased immeasurably during the past century—for all indications are that Dewey would have been delighted by this development, and no doubt would have rewritten the paragraph if its tone was pointed out to him. But there is another point: In fact, Dewey seems to have been mistaken in the claim he was making about these "savages" and their systems of knowledge. He is contrasting the ways in which we and savages respond to the appearance of a comet. We respond by considering the connections this experience has to other items or systems in the web of knowledge we possess; but savages do not do so and lapse into habitual ways of dealing with threatening phenomena—the beating of gongs and so forth. This is very tough on savages! For they also are using the repository of knowledge (and also the technologies) that they have available as a result of earlier experiences—it is just that their knowledge and technologies are less developed than our own. They too are humans, not members of a quite different biological group. It is hard to avoid the conclusion that inadvertently Dewey has himself introduced a breach of continuity here based on a dualism of us versus savages.

And so we head to the finish line.

26

Theories of Morals

Why end "an introduction to philosophy of education" with a chapter on theories of morals or moral philosophy? Because, one hazards a guess, education is a vital activity, on which the very survival of human society depends, and on which the development of individual members of society qua members of their social group also depends. Moral ideas are integral to these vital processes, for they deal with the issue of the proper modes of interaction between individuals within a society. As Dewey put it in the closing paragraph of chapter 7 of *Reconstruction in Philosophy* (written only four years or so after D&E was completed),

> When the identity of the moral process with the processes of specific growth is realized, the more conscious and formal education of childhood will be seen to be the most economical and efficient means of social advance and reorganization, and it will also be evident that the test of all the institutions of adult life is their effect in furthering continued education. . . . The supreme test of all political institutions and industrial arrangements shall be the contribution they make to the all-around growth of every member of society.

Although Dewey does not make the point quite this way, the moral code or codes that flourish within a society are among its "political institutions," and thus—according to him—have to face this same "supreme test." And it should be noted that in holding this general view, whether right or wrong, Dewey certainly was being a consistent pragmatist: I have made the point many times before that for the pragmatist, ideas are plans of action—we evolved the capacity to form ideas in order to provide intelligent guidance for our actions, and this is as true of moral ideas as it is of any others. The function of moral ideas is to guide our actions within the social groups of which we are members. As Dewey writes at the start of section 4 of chapter 26 of D&E, "Morals are as broad as acts which concern our relationships with others. And potentially this includes all our acts, even though their social bearing may not be thought of at the time of performance."

I have opened my commentary on this final chapter of D&E with a passage from a closely parallel chapter from *Reconstruction*, for this slightly later piece is fuller, clearer, and much more readable than the chapter that is our focus here—and so I commend it to you. But let's focus on chapter 26: it is a difficult piece, but it is not written in particularly awkward prose; the problem stems from the fact that Dewey is attempting to get us to look at theories of morals in a fresh, unfamiliar way. He also covers a great deal of territory, and this makes it quite difficult to give a summary of what is going on in this chapter—so, as discretion is the better part of valor, I will not attempt to do so. Instead I will content myself with giving the "gist" of his argument, leaving the details and the myriad important insights to you, the reader, to disentangle for yourself.

It has seemed to me, on my readings of this chapter over the years, that although Dewey opens by briefly discussing a number of closely related dualisms that over time have influenced our thinking about moral ideas, he omits the one that is quite basic and that implicitly he is attacking in this chapter. This is the division or breach of continuity between scientific and practical ideas, on one hand, and moral ideas, on the other; it is a form of what, these days, is sometimes called Hume's fork—the division between truths of fact and truths of reason. The nub is this:

It is generally recognized that scientific and practical ideas are meant to be worked with, and are to be discarded or revised if they are judged to have failed in guiding our actions in dealing with "problematic situations" in the real world. Moral ideas, on the other hand, are often treated as being quite different from this—they are insulated from empirical input. In other words, they are nonrevisable in light of experience, for they are undergirded by reason (or by some authoritative source that is taken as unquestionable)—no matter what havoc attends our acting on the basis of some particular moral precept, we were right to so act, and we are right to be steadfast in our commitment. (Thus, to take a highly charged contemporary example, opponents of abortion regard it as wrong, as a type of murder; it should never be allowed—no matter what the consequences happen to be.) For Dewey, however, there is no break in continuity between moral and empirical or scientific ideas. He says, at the start of section 3, that in discussions of morals

> the value of concrete, everyday intelligence is constantly underestimated, and even deliberately depreciated. Morals is often thought to be an affair with which ordinary knowledge has nothing to do. Moral knowledge is thought to be a thing apart.

However, Dewey does not take my advice and start in this way with a critique of the dualism of truths of fact versus truths of reason! He points out that the "obstruction which meets us" in thinking about morals is the "split" or "division" that goes under various guises—inner versus outer, spiritual versus physical, mind versus world, soul versus body, motive of action versus consequences of action, character versus conduct. Then he adds that "different schools identify morality with either the state of mind or the outer act and results, each in separation from the other." This last statement serves to remind us that when there is a live dualism, each pole has its (uncompromising) devotees; and also, Dewey is setting the stage for a discussion of some moral theories that are situated poles apart. Thus he continues with a brief discussion of some theories that locate the seat of morality internally, in having the right motives or dispositions, these states being regarded as "more real" than the "despised outer world," which was regarded as "morally indifferent." In reaction, Dewey claims that at the other pole various hedonistic or utilitarian theories developed, which held "that the important thing morally is not what a man is inside of his own consciousness, but what he *does*." Ordinary morality, Dewey notes, "is likely to be an inconsistent compromise of both [types of] views."

Given that Dewey accepts the pragmatic theory of ideas being "plans of action," and that a consequence of this theory is that the worth of an idea (even its truth value) is to be judged by how fruitfully it serves to guide our actions in the world, it would seem that he is close to being a utilitarian himself. For a utilitarian holds that the goodness or badness—the moral status—of our actions is determined by their consequences, in particular, by whether they increase the stock of human happiness. (Utilitarianism is what philosophers call a "consequentialist" approach in moral philosophy.) In *Reconstruction* Dewey has this to say about the issue; I quote him at length as his words are informative:

> Upon the whole, utilitarianism has marked the best in the transition from the classic theory of ends and goods to that which is now possible. It had definite merits. It insisted upon getting away from vague generalities, and down to the specific and concrete. It subordinated law to human achievement instead of subordinating humanity to external law. It taught that institutions were made for man and not man for institutions; it actively promoted all issues of reform. It made moral good natural, humane, in touch with the natural goods of life. It opposed unearthly and other worldly morality. ([1948], p. 180)

With all these strong points, why then was utilitarianism not perfect? Because, as Dewey points out,

> it was still profoundly affected in fundamental points by old ways of thinking. It never questioned the idea of a fixed, final and supreme end. . . . Such a point of view treats concrete activities and specific interests not as worth while in themselves, but as mere external means to getting pleasures . . . [thus] making not only virtue but art,

> poetry, religion and the state into mere servile means of attaining sensuous enjoyments. ([1948], pp. 180–81)

In chapter 26 in D&E (at the end of section 3 and elsewhere), Dewey makes the same point, but far less clearly. For example, he lists various traits of an individual that are in themselves valuable moral traits, but which are misconceived when regarded merely as "instrumental goods," as just being means for attaining the fixed intrinsic, "external" end of happiness:

> Open-mindedness, single-mindedness, sincerity, breadth of outlook, thoroughness, assumption of responsibility for developing the consequences of ideas which are accepted, are moral traits. The habit of identifying moral characteristics with external conformity to authoritative prescriptions may lead us to ignore the ethical value of these intellectual attitudes.

And in the long opening paragraph of section 4, Dewey elaborates:

> Morals concern nothing less than the whole character, and the whole character is identical with the man in all his concrete make-up and manifestations. To possess virtue does not signify to have cultivated a few nameable and exclusive traits; it means to be fully and adequately what one is capable of becoming through association with others in all the offices of life.

A similar passage, but with even stronger emotional tone, ends this final chapter.

Having reached this point, however, some readers might join yours truly in feeling somewhat baffled: There are no "fixed or absolute moral ends" such as happiness; but there are numerous traits, such as the ones listed above, which have "ethical value." What gives them this value? Does Dewey mean that reason shows they are fixed and "absolute" ethical values, which would make them similar to the fixed ends he attacks? Surely he does not mean to imply this. Perhaps, then, he means that they are ethical values because some (or many) people do value them? But this is not satisfactory. Whether people desire or admire or value them is irrelevant to the moral point—the moral issue is whether these traits *ought to be desired or admired or valued.* In short, it can be argued that Dewey does not deal adequately with the issue of what characteristics make a trait morally good or morally bad.

However, this may be too hasty—for Dewey has signaled that he treats goodness in social terms, and maybe this resolves the issue. Right at the start of this chapter, I quoted him as stating, in *Reconstruction*, that the "supreme test" of social institutions including value systems is "the contribution they make to the all-around growth of every member of society." And in the concluding paragraph of the final chapter of D&E, he writes:

> This something for which a man must be good is capacity to live as a social member so that what he gets from living with others balances with what he contributes. What he gets and gives as a human being . . . [is] a widening and deepening of conscious life—a more intense, disciplined, and expanding realization of meanings.

As it stands, however, the position sketched here is a form of social relativism that, arguably, still leaves the central moral issue unaddressed. There is little need to remind present-day readers of the existence of fanatical, tightly bound, revolutionary social groups; but it is perhaps necessary to point out that membership of such a group can satisfy the criteria Dewey mentions, including passing the "supreme test." What an individual can get from belonging to a group like this can balance what he contributes, membership can lead to "a more intense, disciplined, and expanding realization of meanings," and, furthermore, the group might allow its members to become all that they are "capable of becoming through association with others." Some cynical readers might even suppose that a community of fanatics that is dedicated (in part) to the development of its members in the ways hinted at meets Dewey's criteria for being classified as a democracy!

Thankfully, Dewey has a way of dealing with the issues raised here—but he waits until chapter 3 of *Experience and Education* (1938) to argue the central moral point in detail. In essence, he picks up on the criterion he mentioned briefly in talking of the "supreme test," and which he also discussed in the important chapter 4 of D&E—namely, the criterion of all-around growth.

Dewey's discussions in 1916 and 1938 are famous, but do not satisfy everyone. Let us focus here on the later account: Dewey is constrained (or perhaps liberated?) by the fact that, given his pragmatic philosophical posture, he cannot appeal to some abstract or transcendental quality to demarcate goodness from badness. He has to provide a naturalistic account, an account that in some way refers to entities or events within our experience of the natural world (for as has often been argued in D&E, it is in this world that our ideas originate and function to direct our actions). So what is the hallmark of goodness? It is nothing other than the capacity to promote continued and all-around *growth* (which of course, means continued education, for as we have seen earlier in D&E, he has identified growth with education). In 1938 he frames the issue in terms of a burglar; he might have had Herman Harrell Horne in mind, for in 1932 the latter wrote that Dewey's discussion in D&E "sets up no adequate distinction between, no working criterion of, good and evil." Horne goes on to say that a band of racketeers meets Dewey's conditions—his prescriptions fit the good and the bad (p. 523). "What then," Horne asks, "is the difference between the two . . . ?" So in 1938 Dewey tries to elucidate in these noteworthy passages from *Experience and Education*:

> The objection made is that growth might take many different directions: a man, for example, who starts out on a career of burglary may grow in that direction. . . . Hence it is argued that "growth" is not enough; we must also specify the direction in which growth takes place, the end towards which it tends. (p. 36)

This is a fair statement of the issue: growth can be in a good direction or in a bad one. What constitutes the difference? Dewey's response is as follows:

> That a man may grow in efficiency as a burglar, as a gangster, or as a corrupt politician, cannot be doubted. But from the standpoint of growth as education and education as growth the question is whether

> growth in this direction promotes or retards growth in general. Does this form of growth create conditions for further growth, or does it set up conditions that shut off the person who has grown in this particular direction from the occasions, stimuli, and opportunities for continuing growth in new directions? (ibid.)

Over the years there have been many readers of Dewey who still find this response to be wanting. The central figure in twentieth-century analytic philosophy of education, R. S. Peters, in a thoughtful and generally appreciative essay on Dewey, described the issue that would not go away in these terms:

> Did not Napoleon or the Marquis de Sade "grow"? Dewey faced this problem in *Experience and Education* and argued that growth in efficiency as a burglar, as a gangster, or as a corrupt politician does not lead to further growth. Growth in general is retarded by such limited forms of growth. This answer did not help him much as many have pointed out, with imaginative sketches of the developing life-styles of burglars, train robbers, etc. What he needed was other criteria by reference to which desirable and undesirable forms of growth could be distinguished. (*John Dewey Reconsidered*, ed. Peters [1977], p. 104)

Dewey may have had an inkling that his argument was not fully compelling, for at the end of his discussion in D&E, he says that he will "leave you to answer these questions" about the direction of growth. Like a good companion, whose task has been to point to issues in Dewey that are worth pondering, I follow his lead and leave the final verdict up to you, the reader. Certainly I have taken his parting words seriously, and for many decades have been seeking my own answer to "these questions," and I freely acknowledge that the quest continues.

Bibliographical Essay

I made the point at the outset that in *Democracy and Education*—and indeed in many if not all his major writings—Dewey eschewed the use of the usual scholarly devices of direct quotation and detailed citation of sources. In this companion I have followed his lead, at least with respect to providing scholarly references—my aim in doing so was to make the text less cluttered and therefore easier to read. But in our contemporary world, a professor cannot easily shrug off the scholarly niceties, and hence this brief essay about my sources.

First, the featured book itself. There are numerous editions of D&E; I myself own three, and use any one of them according to which is nearest to hand. Nowadays there is something to be said for using the version in the collected works of Dewey published by Southern Illinois University Press; it is volume 9 in the series The Middle Works, 1899–1924. This edition has an interesting introduction (written to mark the sixtieth anniversary of the publication of D&E) by the noted philosopher/social theorist Sidney Hook, who at one stage studied with Dewey.

Although I continue to use the most commonly available commercial editions of Dewey's works (I have voluminous marginalia that have accumulated in them), for many readers this series of collected works will, of course, be the most convenient place to locate any of Dewey's writings, including those I have drawn on in this commentary. The dates of their original publication will enable the reader to locate them: "The Reflex Arc Concept in Psychology" (1896), "My Pedagogic Creed" (1897), *The School and Society* (1900/1915), *The Child and the Curriculum* (1902), *How We Think* (1910/1933), *Reconstruction in Philosophy* (1920/1948), *Experience and Nature* (1925/1929), *The Quest for Certainty* (1929), *Logic: The Theory of Inquiry* (1938), and *Experience and Education* (1938). It is worth noting that a convenient joint edition of *The School and Society* and *The Child and the Curriculum* was produced by Phoenix Books, a division of the University of Chicago Press. As for *Reconstruction in Philosophy*, the reader should ensure that the version consulted has the forty-page introduction Dewey wrote for the reprint in 1948. Dewey also wrote an informative intellectual autobiography, "From Absolutism to Experimentalism" (1930). Useful biographical and intellectual analysis of Dewey can of course be found in many sources, but perhaps the most useful places to start are H. S. Thayer, *Meaning and Action: A Critical History of Pragmatism* (1968), and Robert B. Westbrook, *John Dewey and American Democracy* (1991).

A convenient source in which to locate the writings of William James that have been cited—*Talks to Teachers on Psychology* and "Remarks on Spencer's Definition of Mind as Correspondence"—is The Library of America volume *William James: Writings 1878–1899* (1992). Herbert Spencer's influential essays on education have been collected in *Essays on Education* (numerous reprints). The works of several other notable figures that I have cited are available in many editions—Gadamer, Mill, Rousseau, Wittgenstein, among others. (I prefer the translation of Rousseau's *Emile* by Barbara Foxley for the Dent/Everyman edition, for in my view it captures the force and romantic beauty of Rousseau's prose.)

I have to acknowledge, however, that my main source of background material has been my own previous writings. I am only slightly embarrassed by the intellectual version of a selfie that follows, for the fact is I have been writing on the history of nineteenth- and twentieth-century ideas, on the classic pragmatists, and on philosophy of education for about five decades, and it would be extremely odd if I had not learned something. So to proceed . . .

The holistic or organicist position, which stems from Hegel's principle of "internal relations" and which relates to Dewey's attacks on dualisms, is discussed in some detail in *Holistic Thought in Social Science* (1976), and also in chapter 3 of *The Expanded Social Scientist's Bestiary* (2000). A comparison of the ideas of Karl Popper and Dewey, originally published in the journal *Educational Theory* in 1975, is reprinted in the earlier edition of the *Bestiary*, namely, *The Social Scientist's Bestiary* (1992). Paul Hirst, Jerome Bruner, and the "structure of knowledge" theory that influenced curriculum development in many countries are discussed in *Philosophy, Science, and Social Inquiry* (1987). My recent reflections on Dewey's conception of community and democracy are in my 2010 John Dewey Society lecture, "Dealing 'Competently with the Serious Issues of the Day': How Dewey (and Popper) Failed," published in *Educational Theory* (vol. 62, no. 2 [2012]). Detailed background on a number of theorists and theories mentioned in this companion, including John Locke, Jean Piaget, Helvétius, Pestalozzi, the sensationalists, von Baer and the theory of recapitulation, Herbart, Dr. Benjamin Spock, and others, will be found in the book I coauthored with John Cleverley, *Visions of Childhood: Influential Models from Locke to Spock* (1986). Interested readers will also be able to pursue in more depth many topics only touched on in this companion in the two-volume encyclopedia that I recently edited, *The Encyclopedia of Educational Theory and Philosophy* (2014); it includes entries by myself and others on the spectator theory of knowledge, Dewey, James, Mill, Spencer, Hegel, Gadamer, *Bildung*, Herbart, Piaget, Popper, and many more topics.

I also have written at length on the character of the contemporary field of philosophy of education; my most recent effort, with coauthor Harvey Siegel, is the long entry "Philosophy of Education" in the online *Stanford Encyclopedia of Philosophy* (just "google" the encyclopedia's title). Other helpful sources on this topic are Richard Bailey et al., eds., *The SAGE Handbook of Philosophy of Education* (2010); Harvey Siegel, ed., *The Oxford Handbook of Philosophy of Education* (2009); and the textbook by Nel Noddings, *Philosophy of Education* (1995 and subsequent editions).

Finally, as mentioned at the start of this book, when writing was almost complete, I discovered another, long out-of-print companion to D&E, authored by Herman Harrell Horne in 1932. Published by Macmillan (with a reprint in 1944), it had an unwieldy title: *The Democratic Philosophy of Education: Companion to Dewey's "Democracy and Education": Exposition and Comment.* It is a hefty volume, rivaling D&E in size; it mostly consists of lengthy and detailed point-by-point expositions of Dewey's chapters, with much shorter commentaries. The latter reflect Horne's adherence to the philosophy of Absolute Idealism—like the younger Dewey, Horne's orientation had been shaped by Hegel, but unlike Dewey, he maintained this orientation throughout his life. Thus there are many points on which I disagree with him, but some of his criticisms parallel my own.